JUSTICE IN

New Perspectives in Post-Rabbinic Judaism

Series Editor—**Shaul Magid** (Indiana University)

JUSTICE IN THE CITY

Aryeh Cohen

Boston
2013

Library of Congress Cataloging-in-Publication Data:
A catalog record for this title is available from the Library
of Congress.

ISBN 978-1-936235-64-3 (hardback)

ISBN 978-1-618112-96-5 (paperback)

Book design by Ivan Grave

Published by Academic Studies Press in 2013
28 Montfern Avenue
Brighton, MA 02135, USA
press@academicstudiespress.com
www.academicstudiespress.com

Contents

ACKNOWLEDGEMENTS

This book started years ago in conversations at the Progressive Jewish Alliance. I am grateful to Daniel Sokatch for his friendship and camaraderie, for his work at the helm of the PJA, creating a home for creative Jewish thinking and direct action around social justice issues, and for his tireless efforts to create a more just society. I am also grateful to the participants in the short-lived PJA think tank—David Myers, Patsy Ostroy, Joe Ostroy, Eric Greene, Sharon Dolovitch, Jamie Rapaport, Chaim Seidler-Feller and Daniel Sokatch—to whom I presented a very early version of the first part of this book.

The PJA, under the leadership of Elissa Barret and Eric Greene, and Clergy and Laity United for Economic Justice, L.A., under the leadership of Jonathan Klein, have been my activist communities, for which I am grateful.

I want to thank several cohorts of students in my "Issues of Justice" seminar at the Ziegler School for Rabbinic Studies, where I was able to teach much of this material; as well as the rabbinical students (from both Ziegler and HUC) and the business leaders who participated in the seminar on economic justice and Jewish sources that I led together with Bill Cutter, whom I am grateful to also call my friend.

I am very thankful for Gordon Bernat-Kunin's ongoing friendship, intellectual companionship, and the very many pleasurable hours of conversation and hiking in the Santa Monica mountains during which I tried out many of the themes of this book.

Andrea Hodos, Ariella Radwin, Danya Ruttenberg, Jeff Helmreich, Michael Lerner, Elissa Barret, and Michael Berenbaum read the manuscript in whole or in part and I am grateful for their comments and criticism, which have improved it immensely. I am indebted to Michael Berenbaum for his help in many other ways as well. Danya Ruttenberg generously introduced me to the ways of book proposals and agents. Thank you. Bradley Shavit Artson has been a friend and my dean for about the same amount of time. I am grateful for both, and for his commitment to this project.

Charlotte Fonrobert read the complete manuscript more carefully than I could have dared to hope. I am very thankful for her insightful comments.

It is hard to adequately express my gratitude to Shaul Magid. He is a friend, an inspiration, and a collaborator in envisioning a different and better world. Thank you.

The Shtibl Minyan has provided my family and me a warm and loving community within which to sing and learn and do acts of justice and kindness. Thank you.

Neal Castleman has been a friend for a long time, and I am especially thankful for his support through the Castleman Family Foundation for the publication of this book.

Finally, to Andrea, I am so happy that we get to create a life together. Shachar and Oryah, when you need to articulate an intellectual understanding of your deep intuitions about justice, I hope this book might help. I love you all.

Introduction

In this book I argue that the literature of the rabbis—and especially the Babylonian Talmud, the central canonical text of Rabbinic Judaism—paints a compelling picture of what a just city should be. A just city should be a *community of obligation*. That is, in a community thus conceived, the privilege of citizenship is the assumption of the obligations of the city toward others who are not always in view. These "others" include workers, the poor, and the homeless. They form a constitutive part of the city.[1]

The goal of this project is to ground a conception of justice in a tradition of rabbinic discourse centering on the Babylonian Talmud. This theory of justice that I seek to propose is significantly drawn from that textual tradition, while it is also based on a contemporary ethical and philosophical framework. Most prominently, I am indebted to the twentieth-century French Jewish philosopher Emmanuel Levinas for a framework of interpersonal ethics which allows me to see rabbinic ethics more clearly and to ask sharper questions about rabbinic ethics. At the same time, I am indebted to the Babylonian Talmud and the textual tradition it generated to enhance or critique what I consider to be Levinas's asymmetrical obsession with the Other.

Ancient Texts, Contemporary Claims

There are two areas in this work which might encounter resistance in different parts of the audience with which I am engaging. The first is the claim that I can read these texts of late antiquity such that they are relevant to contemporary situations and, even more so, will have some normative weight, and that I can still read them with integrity and academic rigor and discipline. This argument brushes up against a certain type of academic propriety which would claim that there are unbridgeable social, cultural, philosophical, linguistic, and ideological chasms between us and the community of readers for whom and among whom the text was originally written.[2]

The second area of resistance might arise from those who think that the only faithful reading is one in which the reader exhibits certain specific faith commitments. My claim is that although my reading of Rabbinic Judaism in this book certainly makes claims on that tradition, it is not premised on specific faith claims. First things first.

The first argument is that a hermeneutic engagement with the Talmud will yield or generate a claim on our notions of justice which ought to be listened to. The claim is that writing within a tradition brings a certain gravity to an argument that it might not otherwise have. This is not the same as arguing from tradition (saying, for example, that X is old and hoary, and therefore, it is right). Arguing within a tradition brings a certain cultural vocabulary to bear on a problem which is not solved by recourse to first principles.[3]

The hermeneutic engagement itself brings to bear or is itself imminently intertwined with a necessary sociality.[4] Studying together in actuality or theory implicates both author and reader in a process of persuasion which is grounded on a textual moment. When we place a text between us either metaphorically (as in this book) or in actuality (if we were sitting around a table), we engage in an activity one of whose steps is entering into the parameters of a textually bounded moment. There is a notion of a "shared project" in the attempt to understand together or dialogue through the text. This notion is not dissimilar to constitutional interpretation, in that there is a premium placed on the legal interpretation arrived at being grounded in the textual situation (i.e., the Constitution or the Bill of Rights), rather than merely in this or that principled belief. For this type of textual reasoning to take place, the text that is mediating or generating the dialogue (and which, in this specific way, will ultimately ground the interpretation) must be a text that generates a certain level of respect or have at least a patina of gravity. One need not have a declared fidelity to the text (though one might, as in the case of the Constitution), but one must have at least a level of respect for the text.

Through this joint study of a text—in the case of this book, rabbinic texts—I invite you into a discourse on an issue of import without having to develop an argument from first principles. The unfolding of the subsequent dialogue is informed by the fact that it is mediated through a text which is part of a tradition. This connection to tradition brings to bear a certain hermeneutic seriousness which might be called inspirational. By this I mean that in our dialogue, there is an intention to "follow in the footsteps"[5] of the implications of a *sugya* in the Babylonian Talmud, where implications would be arrived at through what might be a generous, though discursively rigorous, reading of that sugya. The sociality of the hermeneutic situation implies that the consequences of the engagement will be, or are intended to be, applied outside this specific engagement.

As a result, this form of interpretation will not be a claim for a literalist reading of texts or an insinuation of (the discourse of) a particular faith commitment into the political and ethical vocabulary of justice. It will rather be a display of the textured use of the vocabulary that the Jewish legal/textual tradition presents. This is itself a goal, since part of the larger exercise is staking a claim to a Judaism which privileges justice and in which justice is the warp and woof of society. That is, I would like to have shown by the end of this book that the discourse of justice that I refer to is not something grafted on to a core religious vocabulary by artificial means, but rather that this discourse of justice is of the essence of that core religious vocabulary. I will have accomplished this by revealing, from within the textual center of Jewish tradition, that vocabulary.

Locating This Book

This book is located in a number of theoretical and actual places. This is a discussion that is located in the city and also, in many ways, a particular city—Los Angeles. This is for both contemporary reasons and historical and traditional reasons. Rabbinic Judaism is an urban phenomenon.[6] While a large proportion of the laws that are discussed in the earliest collections of Jewish law—Mishnah and Tosefta and the commentaries on those works, the Babylonian and Palestinian Talmuds—are agricultural laws, the authors of those collections themselves were urban dwellers. Further, the sages who composed these books, while being embedded in different cultures in many ways, share the fact that they were part of a multiethnic/multireligious urban milieu.[7] So while the sages, especially those of the Babylonian Talmud who will be at the center of our concerns, wrote about (almost literally) everything and everywhere, they were themselves located in an urban environment and saw its concerns as their concerns.

In the cities, in the markets, in the bathhouses, the sages came into contact with people of other religions and ethnicities. This led to competition, polemics, sharing, boundary crossing, and boundary marking.[8] The sages also came into contact with poverty, workers, conflict over wages, prices, ideologies, and practices. The sages wrote about institutional justice and (the problematics of) its application.[9] My working assumption, then, is that there is wisdom which might be extracted from these conversations which can be translated to contemporary realities.

Our contemporary urban centers are places of great conflict and injustice. According to a survey by the Institute for Research on Labor and Employment, "low-wage workers in Los Angeles regularly experience violations of basic laws that mandate a minimum wage and overtime pay and are frequently forced to work off the clock or during their breaks."[10] According to a 2009 study by the National Law Center on Homelessness & Poverty and the National Coalition for the Homeless, Los Angeles was spending $6 million a year to pay for fifty extra police officers to crack down on crime in the Skid Row area at a time when the city budgeted only $5.7 million for homeless services.[11] This becomes all the more startling when one notes that there were nearly fifty thousand homeless people in Los Angeles every night at the time of the study.[12]

Yet this is not, and need not be, the whole story. Megalopolises like Los Angeles, New York, and others—because of their size and the density of their populations—contain great possibilities for creating community and doing justice. An overwhelming number of people live, work, play, and interact with each other in these urban centers. In my lifetime, I will meet a miniscule percentage of the people who share my city with me. However, on a regular basis, I will act in ways that will affect many of those other Angelenos for good or ill. The choices I make as a resident of this polis can lead to more justice and recognition of the others who share my city, or they can lead in the opposite direction.

This book, to some extent, is an attempt to flesh out Emmanuel Levinas's notion of a "humane urbanism."[13] I read this generally to mean a practice of living such that I am attentive to the consequences—immediate and ultimate—of my actions upon those whom I do not know but who share this city with me.

Levinas states the goal of his philosophical exploration as "maintaining, within anonymous community, the society of the I with the Other—language and goodness."[14] This dense statement is the translation of his philosophical insight into the working of the polis. The goal is to see the interactions between people—between the I and the Other, or between myself and another person—within an anonymous community, as sites or moments of justice. For Levinas, it is coming face-to-face with the other person, which is referred to here as "language," which removes the Other from anonymity and instills an obligation on the part of the I toward the Other—this is referred to here as "goodness."[15]

One of the important things to note here is that the reason Levinas speaks of the "I" and the "Other" rather than "myself and another person" is to distinguish between the two people in a complete way. The basic characteristic of another person is that she is not me—that is, she is not the same as me; and therefore, also, I am not able to glibly understand her as a slight variant of me. This is what Levinas refers to as the philosophical mistake of assimilating the Other into the Same.

Navigating those anonymous interactions justly is dependent upon my recognition that the Other is beyond my grasp and my ability to completely understand, assimilate, and, especially, make use of or exploit. This leaves me only the ability to listen to, to hear, to learn from, or to be commanded by the Other. I am deprived of the ability to control, to own, to enslave. In an anonymous community, in a non-intimate relationship with the many people whom I don't "know," I am still obliged to maintain this society with the Other. My obligation to the Other is forced upon me by my recognition of my asymmetrical relationship with another person—the Other is transcendent. This latter idea is somewhat counterintuitive to the current ethos of American culture. The political culture of the United States is a culture of rights, while the popular culture is a culture of individual expression and entitlement.[16] Levinas's understanding of the relationship between the self and the Other is a relationship of obligation—that is, I am obligated to the Other person from the moment of the first meeting or interaction.

I, therefore, need to recognize, to understand, and to be attentive to the ways in which my actions affect those parts of the larger anonymous community with which I am not in intimate contact. I must act politically (that is, as a member of the polis) in a manner which flows from my obligation to that larger anonymous community which is not "I" nor the same as "I." Finally, I must curtail the reach of those actions which come from a perspective in which I think that I can completely grasp the strangers in my city whom I don't know and place them into the neat categories that I already have. At the same time, I must expand those actions which respond to those strangers as complete human beings beyond my ability to completely understand.

My thinking in this book is in line with contemporary thinkers who might take as their motto the subtitle of a recent book by Kwame Anthony Appiah, *Ethics in a World of Strangers*.[17] The world I am focused on right now is the major urban center I inhabit—and similar ones inhabited by millions in many locations in the world.

The City in the Philosophical Tradition

In the Greek philosophical tradition, beginning with Plato in *The Republic* and continuing with Aristotle in *Politics*,[18] the city was understood in the context of virtue ethics. The point of a city was to enable all the excellences of all the virtues to come together in one place. This was a result of Plato's claim that any one person could only excel at or perfect one virtue or skill from youth. If there was to be perfection of all the virtues, there would need to be a collection of people who together as a whole would perfect all the virtues. As Averroes, the thirteenth-century Muslim Spanish philosopher, paraphrased Plato's argument:

> It . . . appears that no man's substance can become realized through any of these virtues unless [a number of] humans help him and that to acquire his virtue a man has need of other people. Hence he is political by nature.[19]

Averroes explains that cities exist for one of three reasons: (1) There is an unavoidable necessity. In other words, the only way that many people can acquire the stuff of survival (food, clothing, etc.) is by banding together and mutually supporting each other. (2) Cities are easier. In cities, not everybody has to learn how to plant or sew or make pottery. People can benefit from the skills that others have. (3) It is the best way. "Since it is impossible that the human perfections be attained other than in different individuals within a given population, the individuals of this species are all different in natural disposition corresponding to the difference in their perfections. . . . [T]his being as we have characterized it, there ought to exist an association of humans—[an association] perfect in every species of human and [whose members] are helped to their completion in that the less perfect follows the fully perfect by way of preparing for his own perfection, and the more perfect aids the less by giving him the principles of his perfection."[20]

This last reason, unsurprisingly, is the most important reason for the Aristotelian tradition. That is, a city is an association in which people assemble to aid each other in perfecting their individual virtues, and then the city as a whole will be perfect in its virtues.

Finally, the city will be considered a just city, according to Plato, when each person pursues that activity to which he is disposed by nature. Justice is the "equity" that results when "every one of them [i.e., the citizens] will perform the activity that is his by nature and will not long for what does not belong to him. This being so, this city will be just in their associating together in it, for the equity in it consists only in every one of its citizens doing what is singularly his."[21]

Justice in the city, ultimately, for this tradition, is both a means toward and a reflection of the virtue of justice in an individual. Justice is based on the notion that each person has a specific nature which is immutable and must be perfected within its unique disposition. Finally, this mode of philosophizing starts from the question: "Why do people congregate in cities?" The method of thinking is to imagine an ideal city (which, it is conceded, is not like any city that is known) toward which our cities should aim.[22]

This approach, which invokes a thought experiment constructing an ideal city in order to decide what actual cities should be like, has a long trajectory. It is found throughout the Middle Ages and down to the contract theorists of the nineteenth century and on to the late twentieth century in philosophers, such as John Rawls and his *Theory of Justice*, which imagines an "original situation" in which people behind a "veil of ignorance" decide what the appropriate mix of benefits and deficits in wealth and poverty, hunger and plenty, etc., should be in the ideal city.[23]

A major distinction between the city of this philosophical tradition and the city of rabbinic literature is that the latter is grounded in the concrete reality of actual human interaction. The existence of cities is a given. There is no attempt made to imagine the city of the philosophical imagination, to construct an ideal city out of whole cloth.[24] The purpose of rabbinic legislation is to start with the cities as given and move them in the direction of justice. A city needs a court;[25] a city needs a social safety net;[26] a city must provide food and shelter for wayfarers.[27] The city is the mediating element of the obligations of individuals. In a way, this is a revolution of thought whose origins were in the demands placed on individuals for poverty relief in the Torah. These individual demands, if aggregated, could become a loose safety net. The genius of the rabbis was to institutionalize and universalize the demands. A pauper looking for relief in the city of the Torah's imagination would easily find that relief if she was lucky enough to be living in a rural and highly agrarian area. The city-born-and-bound poor would be highly disadvantaged when trying to collect their share of the gleanings from the few fields in the urban orbit.

The rabbis moved beyond the idea of a city as the mechanism by which individuals could fulfill their obligations to others, to an idea of the city as being the locus of obligation, whose burden was shared by all residents. The social safety net (food, clothing, shelter) was an obligation of the *city*.[28] The city, through its institutions and representatives, passed that obligation on to its residents. It is in the legal construction of this web of interpersonal responsibility, which is backed up with the force of both moral and legal authorities, that the just city, the community of obligation, emerges.

While there are many important differences between the rabbinic city and the Aristotelian *polis*, using the term *polis* allows me to use the terms politics and political in a way which conveys commitment to the ideals of a community of obligation rather than the degraded understanding that the word has assumed in contemporary culture.

The Rabbinic Textual Tradition and This Book

This work is intellectually and spiritually located in the rabbinic textual tradition, and especially the articulation of that tradition in the Babylonian Talmud. By this, I mean two things. First, the conceptual frame which I develop in this book emerges from a close and diligent reading of texts in the Babylonian Talmud (called *sugyot*). This is not an exercise in selective quotation of seemingly sympathetic or noxious lines, but rather a reading of arguably complete discussions. It is the reading itself which reveals the conceptual frame. It is then in this type of thick analysis that the conceptual vocabulary of *Justice in the City* will come to light, rather than being found in the occasional saying or anecdote.

Rabbinic thought can also serve as a critique of Levinas's radical focus on my obligation to the other. For Levinas, obligation is not mutual; it is asymmetrical. There is no serial order of obligation (even though you would see me as hierarchically elevated, as I do you). I do not respond to you because I expect that you would respond to me in the future. While this is powerful when I think about my obligations to others and to the Stranger (even *our* obligation to the Stranger), it is disempowering from the point of view of the Other. If obligation is what defines me as a member of the polis, what defines the one to whom I am obligated as a member of the polis? As I will demonstrate, the sages of the Mishnah and the Talmud are very clear on this point. Since all are defined as persons based on obligation, all are obligated—even the poor must give charity, etc. The community of obligation that I envision is one in which all of its members are obligated.

The Personal

This book is also located in my own intellectual biography. Although I am profoundly interested in philosophy, I am not trained as a philosopher. I am a Talmudist by training, having studied in both traditional settings (Yeshivot) and universities. While I have in almost every sense left the world of the Yeshivot, I still carry the bias toward thinking through texts which I grew up with in the *batei midrash*, study halls, of my youth and young adulthood. At the same time, one of the reasons that I left the world of the Yeshivot was so that I could think critically about the biases of the texts.

I teach in a seminary which trains men and women for the Conservative rabbinate. This means that I am challenged on a daily basis to articulate the connection between the texts I am teaching and the people "out there" to whom my charges will minister. "How is this relevant?" I am often asked. Often the best and most appropriate response is to deflect the question—to teach my students to listen to the text as "commanding Other" before immediately attempting wholesale pastoral transvaluation. However, I am also invested in my students, future rabbis, being able to think about and articulate to their eventual congregants, colleagues, and fellow citizens, the obligations that devolve upon them from being part of a polis. I think in Jewish terms about these obligations and would hope that my students would too.

In addition to my practice in the academy, I am also a social justice activist who has held (and still holds) leadership positions in Jewish and interfaith social justice organizations (the Progressive Jewish Alliance or PJA and Clergy and Laity United for Economic Justice or CLUE). My involvement in the Jewish social justice movement has allowed me to combine my academic practice with the practice of organizing and advocating in the streets. I was instrumental in the creation of the Jewish Community Justice Project, a restorative justice project which mediated between first- or second-time nonviolent offenders and those who were hurt by their offenses. I was part of a group that wrote and submitted amicus or "friend of the court" briefs in which we articulated an objection from within a progressive Jewish position to the death penalty, to trying minors as adults, and to other issues. I participated in the Justice for Janitors campaign, writing a letter outlining the responsibilities of employers to their workers and workers to their employers in the Jewish tradition. Ultimately, tens of rabbis from Southern California signed the letter, and it was instrumental in winning a union contract from one of the largest mall owners in the country. I went with interfaith delegations of clergy to managements in support of hotel workers, security workers, and grocery workers. I participated in civil disobedience and was arrested while supporting hotel workers' demands for a fair and just contract.

Being on both the front lines and in the study hall sharpened my sense of the need for an articulated Jewish view of justice, drawn from the heart of the textual tradition. I was not satisfied with the oft-cited verses which traditionally decorate the banners and placards at protests and demonstrations. I began by developing curricula and articulating positions in papers that I shared with my academic colleagues at conferences and my activist partners in a nascent think tank at the PJA. I started developing a course to teach to my rabbinic students and ultimately developed a joint course with Bill Cutter of the Hebrew Union College for rabbinic students of both our institutions, and CEOs of companies in Los Angeles, on issues of economic justice in the Jewish textual tradition. The logical endpoint of that activity is this book—a textured and grounded Jewish account of certain principles of social justice in an urban setting.

The Order of the Book

The book is organized along the following lines. The first three chapters draw out three fundamental principles of justice in the city. Chapter 1's bottom line is concisely articulated as "Choose to be like God and not like Pharaoh." This chapter discusses the obligation to create our urban spaces so that we are able to hear the cry of the poor. The chapter analyzes a text from Tractate Baba Bathra and the commentary upon it in the Babylonian Talmud. This involves stories about Elijah, the prophet, and the sages he comes to visit. Ultimately, the challenge posed by the first principle is to live in the city such that you are available to hear your neighbor—whom you do not know—in her moment of despair, so that you can act in a manner that is just.

The second chapter argues for the obligation of dissent. If cities should ultimately be comprised of webs of just relationships between strangers, one incurs an obligation to protest against injustice at any place along those webs. This chapter analyzes a Talmudic story which supplies a counterexample to protesting injustice, and investigates the way that that story was dealt with in the commentary tradition.

The third chapter argues that the boundaries of responsibility of one who lives in an urban setting extend far beyond the geographical boundaries of one's home and neighborhood and specific community. I argue that the boundaries of obligation of necessity encompass all who live in the city, and that I am obligated to make the ramifications (even the distant ramifications) of my actions occasions of justice.

An important corollary of this principle is that it extends not only beyond my geographical space and the community therein—implicitly arguing against an ethic of intimacy or hospitality—but beyond my religious community.

The second part of the book engages specific areas of social justice.

Chapter 4 addresses the issue of homelessness. I trace the obligation to house the homeless in the textual tradition as it moves from an individual obligation, impinging on certain absolute property rights, to a communal obligation, as a recognized "need of the poor." At the same time, I argue that homelessness itself subverts the very idea of a city as a community of obligation.

Chapter 5 addresses labor. Relationships between employers and employees play out much differently when framed in an ethic of obligation. This approach is neither market based nor classically socialist. The question of the value of labor and the worth and dignity of the laborer is central to rabbinic discussions. In this chapter, I argue that the community has an obligation to intervene in the market to ensure that the distinction between wage labor and slave labor is bright and wide. The "market" is not a natural force in the world, but rather a long and involved series of choices made by individuals. At each juncture, one can choose justly or unjustly. When decisions about labor are made from the point of view of the community and its obligations to justice, one cannot hide behind the screen of "market forces" or "the demands of Wall Street."

If one were to operate within the principles I have argued for, one would then have to rethink the justice system along the lines of restorative rather than punitive justice. This is the subject of the sixth chapter. If the goal of a system of justice is to restore to wholeness the web of relationships that were rent by the actions of a person who disregarded his or her obligations to others, then the end of that system would not be punishment but "restoration." Restoration would include both compensation and (in many cases) some form of punishment (especially in cases of violence in which the offender either is still a threat or has proven himself or herself unable to participate in a just community), but ultimately the goal would be to restore the community. Restorative justice, as I understand it, is based on two principles. The first is that human character is corrigible and not immutable. The second claim is that justice is dependent on the recognition of the dignity of everyone in the community.

A Short Primer on Rabbinic Literature for the Uninitiated

When, in this book, I refer to the rabbis or a specific rabbi (or equally, when I refer to a sage or the sages), I refer not to a contemporary cleric, but rather to a member of the intellectual and spiritual guild which flourished in the first seven or so centuries of the first millennium and which created Rabbinic Judaism. (Rabbinic Judaism is, for all intents and purposes, the archetype for every contemporary Judaism from right to left.)

The central texts of the rabbinic canon are the Mishnah, the Tosefta, the Palestinian Talmud, and the Babylonian Talmud. The Mishnah is arguably the first text of Rabbinic Judaism. It was published in the first part of the third century of the Common Era. It is a collection of legal statements which might be a law code or a legal textbook or a casebook. This is still being debated. The Tosefta is an alternative version of Mishnah published either before it or as a commentary to it. None of the classical texts of Judaism come with a real introduction, so some of the basic meta-questions about them are not answered or cannot be answered.[29]

The Palestinian Talmud is a commentary on most of Mishnah. It was finished in the fourth or fifth century and consists of legal discussions of the Mishnah and, at times, the Tosefta. It also has material which is not directly connected to either the Mishnah or the Tosefta, but to its own legal or theological agenda.

The seventh-century Babylonian Talmud is the crown jewel of rabbinic texts and has been the cornerstone of the traditional Jewish curriculum from as early as the tenth century. The Babylonian Talmud is a sprawling work which is comprised of law, legal theory, religious discourse, and folk wisdom, and uses the commentary form often as the pretext for excursions which go far afield, following an internal logic. The Babylonian Talmud has also generated a voluminous commentary tradition which began soon after its completion and continues to this day.

Notes

[1] For this reason, in this work, I use the Greek term *polis* interchangeably with *city* and identify the latter as a community of obligation. A *polis* denotes not only a randomly assembled mass of humans who by chance live together. A *polis* in the Greek sense is the end result of a natural tendency of humans to congregate and create communities. A person, in the Aristotelian philosophical tradition, is a *zoon politikon*, a political being.

[2] See, for example, Miriam B. Peskowitz, *Spinning Fantasies: Rabbis, Gender and History* (University of California Press, 1997), pp. 154–177, esp. 171: "Our modern ways of making the past make meaning offer no salvation and little redemption. Relations with the past are never innocent. They are always gendered, and often with ill effects."

[3] This is not the same as Alisdair Macintyre's notion of tradition. Cf. *Whose Justice? Whose Rationality?*, esp. chapter 18. See also Moshe Helinger, "Justice and Social Justice in Halakhic Judaism and in Current Liberal Thought" (Heb.) in Yedidia Z. Stern, ed. *My Justice, Your Justice: Justice across Cultures* (The Zalman Shazar Center, the Israel Democracy Institute, 2010), 111–145. Helinger's fine article is marred by his felt need to distance himself from unnamed "contemporary Jewish liberal understandings which often bend before the liberal norms without sufficient critique of that position" (p. 125). This is especially unfortunate since he must know that there are those who would apply this same critique to his own "personal" reading of the Jewish political tradition. For a different approach to bringing Talmudic discussions to bear on contemporary issues, see Gerald J. Blidstein, "Talmudic Ethics and Contemporary Problematics," *Review of Rabbinic Judaism* 12.2 (2009): 204–217.

[4] Robert Gibbs, "Verdict and Sentence: Cover and Levinas on the Robe of Justice" in *Journal of Jewish Thought and Philosophy*, vol. 14, no. 1–2 (2006): 73–90.

[5] Cf. Edith Wyschogrod, *Saints and Postmodernism: Revisioning Moral Philosophy*, especially chapter 1.

[6] Cf. Charlotte Elisheva Fonrobert, "The Political Symbolism of the Eruv," *Jewish Social Studies* 11, no. 3 (2005): 9–35; Alan Segal, *Rebecca's Children: Judaism and Christianity in the Roman World* (Harvard University Press, 1986).

[7] Fergus Millar, *The Roman Near East: 31 BC–AD 337* (Harvard University Press, 1994).

[8] Cf. Galit Hasan-Rokem, *Tales of the Neighborhood: Jewish Narrative Dialogues in Late Antiquity* (Ewing, NJ: University of California Press, 2003); Daniel Boyarin, *Border Lines: The Partition of Judaeo-Christianity* (University of Pennsylvania, 2004).

[9] Cf. Beth A. Berkowitz, *Execution and Invention: Death Penalty Discourse in Early Rabbinic and Christian Cultures* (Oxford University Press, 2006).

[10] Ana Luz Gonzalez Ruth Milkman, Victor Narro, *Wage Theft and Workplace Violations in Los Angeles: The Failure of Employment and Labor Law for Low-Wage Workers* (UCLA Institute for Research on Labor and Employment, 2010), 1.

[11] "Homes Not Handcuffs: The Criminalization of Homelessness in U.S. Cities" (The National Law Center on Homelessness & Poverty and the National Coalition for the Homeless, 2009): 33.

[12] "2009 Greater Los Angeles Homeless Count Report" (Los Angeles Homeless Services Authority, 2009).

[13] The term is found in his essay "Cities of Refuge," which appears in the collection *Beyond the Verse: Talmudic Readings and Lectures* (Athlone Press, 1994).

[14] Emmanuel Levinas, *Totality and Infinity: An Essay on Exteriority*, translated by Alphonso Lingis, (Duquesne University Press, 1969), 47.

[15] Levinas's claim is actually stronger. He claims that "Desire," whose essence is murderous of the Other, "becomes, faced with the other, and 'against all good sense,' the impossibility of murder" of the Other (ibid.).

[16] For one of a plethora of examples, see Rob Walker, *The Born Identity*, http://www.nytimes.com/2010/08/01/magazine/01fob-consumed-t.html. (A version of this article appeared in print on August 1, 2010, on page MM19 of the New York Times magazine).

[17] Kwame Anthony Appiah, *Cosmopolitanism: Ethics in a World of Strangers* (W. W. Norton, 2006).

[18] By the Middle Ages, these were read as complementing each other. See *Averroes on Plato's Republic*, translated, with an introduction and notes by Ralph Lerner (Cornell University Press, 1974).

[19] Averroes, *Averroes on Plato's Republic*, translated, with an introduction and notes (Cornell University Press, 1974), 5. Cf. "It follows that the state belongs to the class of objects which exist by nature, and that man is by nature a political animal." Aristotle, *Politics*, I.253.a1.

[20] Ibid., 6.

[21] Ibid., 53.

[22] Cf. "Since we see that every city-state is a sort of community and that every community is established for the sake of some good (for everyone does everything for the sake of what they believe to be good), it is clear that every community aims at some good, and the community which has the most authority of all and includes all the others aims highest, that is, at the good with the most authority. This is what is called the city-state or political community." Aristotle, *Politics*, I.1.1.252a1-7 translation from Fred Miller, "Aristotle's Political Theory," The Stanford Encyclopedia of Philosophy (Spring 2010 Edition), Edward N. Zalta (ed.), URL = http://plato.stanford.edu/archives/spr2010/entries/aristotle-politics/.

[23] Rawls's *Theory of Justice* is of course not just another contractarian theory,

but the most important contemporary restatement of the theory. The discussion and use of Rawls's theory abound. See, for example, Martha C. Nussbaum, *Frontiers of Justice: Disability, Nationality and Species Membership* (Harvard University Press, 2007). The book is dedicated, "In memory of John Rawls." Nussbaum writes: "I have singled out Rawls's theory for critical examination because it is the strongest political theory in the social contract tradition that we have, and, indeed, one of the most distinguished theories in the Western tradition of political philosophy" (p. ix).

[24] One could make the argument that there is an attempt at creating the "anti-city" or the model of the unjust city in the representations of Sodom in Rabbinic literature. See, for example, Genesis Rabbah 49:6 or Mekilta deRabbi Ishamael Tractate Shirata 2.

[25] b Sanhedrin 56b.

[26] Tosefta Peah 4:9.

[27] Mishnah Peah 8:7.

[28] The subject of the verb *ayn pohatin*/"should be given not less than" in Mishnah Peah 8:7 is the *city* as a whole rather than any specific individual. ("A poor man that is journeying from place to place *should be given not less than . . .*")

[29] For the most recent entries in this debate, see Judith Hauptman, *Rereading the Mishnah: A New Approach to Ancient Jewish Texts* (Mohr Siebeck, 2005) and Shamma Friedman, *Tosefta Atikata 'al Masechet Pesach Rishon* (Heb.) (Ramat Gan, 2003).

PART I

Chapter 1

Acting Like Pharaoh or Acting Like God

I believe you to be a person who would hide me if it came to that.
Wouldn't you? Whoever I am or happen to be.
Who would remove the wood planks in the floor, in the
ceiling, let me in to enough breathing space. A person who
will not walk by the man old enough to be your grandfather,
somebody's grandfather, on the street, in this great cold.

Jorie Graham[1]

The biblical book of Exodus tells one of the most powerful tales in the history of the world. The story of the ancient Israelites' redemption from Egypt has generated two blockbuster movies, in addition to supplying the conceptual frame for liberation movements around the world. The scene of Moses splitting the Red Sea while Pharaoh and the Egyptians drown therein almost became the Great Seal of the fledgling United States of America. John Adams recorded this plan for the seal in his own hand in a note dated August 1776, preserved in the archive of the Library of Congress:[2]

> Pharaoh sitting in an open chariot, a crown on his head and a sword in his hand passing through the Red Sea in pursuit of the Israelites: rays from a pillar of fire in the cloud, expression of the divine presence . . . Moses stands on the shore and extending his hand over the sea, causes it to overwhelm Pharaoh. Motto: Rebellion to tyrants is obedience to God.[3]

As a high school student in New York in the early 1970s, I was passionately involved in the movement to save Soviet Jewry. The motto of our struggle was "Let My People Go."[4]

The exodus of the Israelites from Egypt is a tale of redemption. It is also a tale of the possibility of redemption. This is arguably the reason that the yearly ritual enactment and retelling of the story in the Jewish tradition at the Passover Seder is so powerful. The concluding blessing of the liturgical retelling of the exodus at the

Passover Seder invokes the redemption from Egypt as a harbinger of the future and final redemption.

What, then, does the Exodus mean? Even if we were to narrowly define the word "mean," we would not be able to begin to sketch an answer to this question. On the other hand, an achievable goal will be to point to one way the rabbinic tradition understands that the Torah inscribes the Exodus experience in law. Focusing on the familiar passage in the book of Exodus chapter 22, about caring for the alien and the widow, I will point to an unfamiliar reading delineated in the medieval Torah commentary of the thirteenth-century Spanish sage Nachmanides (Rabbi Moshe ben Nachman). In short, I will argue that the Torah does not understand that the lesson of oppression (i.e., slavery in Egypt) is compassion (i.e., for the alien and the widow).[5] The Torah argues, rather, that there is an obligation to imitate the God of the Exodus and not to imitate Pharaoh. This generates other obligations which will become known in the fullness of this essay.

In the second part of the chapter, I will suggest that a certain understanding of the redemptive power of justice is already present in early rabbinic literature. As an example of this, I will examine a short legal discussion in the seventh-century Babylonian Talmud which is informed by a certain reading of the Exodus story as portrayed above.

Exodus and the Cry

Exodus chapter 2 ends at the moment before the commissioning of Moses as redeemer and leader of Israel. Israel is enslaved and suffering under the yoke of bondage and, in its struggles, cries out.

> 23 And it came to pass in the course of those many days that the king of Egypt died; and the children of Israel sighed by reason of the bondage, and they cried, and their cry came up unto God by reason of the bondage.
> 24 And God heard their groaning, and God remembered His covenant with Abraham, with Isaac, and with Jacob.

> 25 And God saw the children of Israel, and God took cognizance of them.

At the end of the chapter, the reader is left with the knowledge that "God took cognizance of" Israel. The reader has no idea what this will lead to yet. This moment itself, however, is the moment at which the redemption story begins. God is now, by virtue of hearing the cries of the slaves, involved and invested.

On a parallel track, Moses has discovered his Israelite identity—earlier in chapter 2—and has fled to Midian to escape the wrath of Pharaoh after killing an Egyptian taskmaster. Moses, too, has seen the oppression of bondage, but he has no idea that he can do anything about it.

The power of this liminal moment—this moment whose place is immediately after knowledge and immediately preceding action—comes from the fact that God will act as a direct result of having heard the cry (*za'akah*) of the children of Israel. God knows or "takes cognizance" (*yada*) because God *heard* their cries and then *remembered* the covenant. This moment leads to—and perhaps enables—redemption.

In the next moment (chapter 3), Moses wanders into God, as it were, and God commissions Moses to take the Israelites out of Egypt.

> 7 And the LORD continued, "I have marked well the plight of My people in Egypt and have heeded their outcry because of their taskmasters; yes, I am mindful of their sufferings.
> 8 I have come down to rescue them from the Egyptians . . ."

God articulates the explicit causality between being attentive to—"hearing"—the cries of the oppressed, and doing something about it—acting on it.

Exodus 5 presents an opposite paradigm. In Moses's first confrontation with Pharaoh, Pharaoh is completely recalcitrant. Pharaoh denies both Moses's request and God's power to back it up. Moses leaves and Pharaoh, as punishment, orders that the Israelite slaves work harder and make the same number of bricks without being given straw. The Israelite foremen appeal then to Pharaoh— they cry out to him. His reaction is the opposite of God's reaction. Pharaoh does not hear.

> 15 Then the foremen of the Israelites came to Pharaoh and cried (*va-yitz'aku*): "Why do you deal thus with your servants?
> 16 No straw is issued to your servants, yet they demand of us: Make bricks! Thus your servants are being beaten, when the fault is with your own people."
> 17 He replied, "You are shirkers, shirkers! That is why you say, 'Let us go and sacrifice to the LORD.'
> 18 Be off now to your work! No straw shall be issued to you, but you must produce your quota of bricks!"

The Israelites *cry out* to Pharaoh (as the Israelites earlier cried out to God), yet Pharaoh turns a deaf ear to their cries. He makes them work harder for crying out. This volitional deafness is answered with ten plagues, the devastation of Egypt, and the exodus of the Israelite slaves.

The redemption from Egypt is inscribed in many of the Torah's laws. It is given as a reason for such disparate laws as keeping the Sabbath (Deut. 5:15) on the one hand and for redeeming the firstborn of one's own loins and one's animals' (Exod. 13:15). These rituals commemorating the Exodus are, in a sense, repayment— God did not kill your firstborn when God slaughtered the Egyptian first-born; and you, therefore, have an obligation of gratitude to sanctify your firstborn to God.[6] I am suggesting that this narrative moment—God's recognition of Israel's suffering and therefore acting on that recognition—is also commemorated and codified in the legal canons of Exodus.

Exodus 22 records a law familiar to all who toil in the vineyard of social justice grounded in biblical religion.

> 20 Do not mistreat an alien or oppress him, for you were aliens in Egypt.
> 21 Do not take advantage of a widow or an orphan.
> 22 If you do and they cry out to me (*tza'ok yitz'ak*), I will certainly hear their cry (*tza'akato*).

23 My anger will be aroused, and I will kill you with the
sword; your wives will become widows and your
children fatherless.

What is the relation between the first and second half of verse 20? What does it mean that you shall not oppress the stranger or
the alien because you were strangers in the land of Egypt? Many
have understood this verse as meaning that the lesson of oppression
is compassion.[7] That is, "You Israelites know what it means to be
enslaved, to be oppressed, to be the stranger. Now that you are the
dominant group, you must exercise compassion towards those who
are like you were. You must exercise the compassion that Pharaoh
did not exercise towards you."

This understanding, however, does not take into account
verse 22. What does your experience of oppression in Egypt have to
do with the fact that if you do not hear, they will cry out to God and
God will hear them—and kill you?

I suggest that Exodus 22:20–23 is memorializing the narrative
of the Exodus which we sketched out above in the law. On the one
hand, God heard the cry of the Israelites, and this led to redemption.
On the other hand, Pharaoh did not hear the cry, and this led to the
devastation of Egypt. The ethical choice is between *imitatio dei* (being
like God) and *imitatio pharaoh* (being like Pharaoh). As is the wont
of the biblical authors, these choices bring with them repercussions.
Choosing to be like God leads to redemption, while choosing to be
like Pharaoh leads to death.

Nachmanides puts this starkly.

> **For you were strangers in the land of Egypt.** [. . .] What is
> correct, in my understanding, is that [God] says "you shall
> not wrong a stranger or oppress him" and think that he has
> no one to save him from your hands, for you know that you
> were strangers in the land of Egypt and I saw the manner
> in which the Egyptians oppressed you (cf. Exod. 3:9) and I
> wreaked vengeance upon them, for I see "the tears of the
> oppressed with none to comfort them; and the power of
> their oppressors—with none to comfort them." (Eccles. 4:1)
> I, however, save all people from those stronger than them
> (cf. Ps. 35:10). So, too, "you shall not ill-treat any widow or
> orphan" (Exod. 22:21), for I will hear their cries, for all these

people do not have faith in themselves, but they can have faith in Me.

In another verse He added an explanation: "For you know the feelings of the stranger, having yourselves been strangers in the land of Egypt." (Exod. 23:9) In other words, you understand that any stranger's soul is humbled, and he groans and cries out, and his eyes are constantly upon God, and He will have mercy on him as He had mercy upon you, as it is written: "The Israelites were groaning under the bondage and cried out; and their cry for help from the bondage rose up to God." (Exod. 2:23) In other words, not by their merit but only because God had mercy on them as a result of the bondage.

The lesson of the slavery and liberation in Egypt is not an exhortation to dwell on shared victimization. This, Nachmanides writes, is an "added explanation." Even the empathy of shared suffering is useful only for another purpose. "Do not think," the Torah tells us, "that the stranger is powerless; that she has no one to come to her aid; that 'he has no one to save him from your hands.' Your experience in Egypt proved that wrong, for when Pharaoh and the Egyptians ignored you and did not hear your cries, 'I saw the manner in which the Egyptians oppressed you.'" It is not the empathy of shared suffering which is at stake here, but the certain knowledge that God hears the cries of those whom others wish to ignore—and who benefit thereby from their continued exploitation. If you will not hear their cries or if you will oppress them and thereby cause their crying out, God will hear them; they *will* be redeemed, but you will be punished. Nachmanides teaches us that the experience we share with all marginal, oppressed, or exploited people is the possibility of redemption. The Torah puts this starkly, to quote Eldridge Cleaver: "What we're saying today is that you're either part of the solution, or you're part of the problem." You can choose to be like God and hear the cries of the oppressed, or you can choose to be like Pharaoh and ignore those cries. In either event, the oppressed will be redeemed. If, however, the salvation is left to God, you will go the way of the Egyptians.

This ethic of hearing, the statement that hearing the cry of the oppressed is the beginning of redemption, finds its way into the rabbinic legal tradition. I am going to show how this understanding will help us make sense of a somewhat challenging Talmudic text.

The Gatehouse

The third-century CE legal text known as the Mishnah covers all areas of law from prayer to torts to sacrifices to the structure of the legal system. Mishnah is the first compilation of rabbinic law and stands as the cornerstone of the Jewish legal tradition.[8] The Mishnah generated two major commentaries—the fifth-century Palestinian Talmud and the seventh-century Babylonian Talmud.[9] Of interest to us here is a law that is found in the first chapter of the last part of the Mishnah tractate, "Torts"/*nezikin*, known as *Baba Bathra*, or the "last gate."[10]

The Mishnah is as follows:

> They may coerce him to [participate in the] building of
> a gate house and a gate for the [joint] courtyard.
> Rabban Shimon ben Gamliel says, Not all courtyards need a
> gate house.

The law states that if people are living in houses that share a common courtyard, the residents of those houses can decide to build a gate and/or a gatehouse for the courtyard; and furthermore, they can force everyone to chip in for the cost of said gate and gatehouse. This is somewhat similar to a contemporary condominium situation in which the owner(s) of one apartment can be forced to pay for certain improvements to the house.

The Babylonian Talmud comments on this Mishnah:

> This implies that the building of a gate house is a laudable
> thing.
> However, there is [the story of] that righteous person
> whom Elijah spoke with [regularly].
> He built a gate house for his house,
> And Elijah no longer spoke with him.

The Babylonian Talmud begins its comment by drawing a straightforward implication from the Mishnah's law. Since the

Mishnah stated that a resident of the shared courtyard could be coerced into sharing the financial burden of building the gatehouse, it is reasonable to assume that building a gatehouse is a laudable thing. The only assumption that one needs to accede to is that the law would not promote behavior which is not "laudable." This seems to be a reasonable assumption.

The Talmud derives this assumption for the purpose of challenging it. The first line is a setup for the inquiry that is to follow. If the building of a gatehouse is a laudable thing, the Talmud asks, why is it then that Elijah stopped his meetings with the righteous person after the latter built a gatehouse?[11] The conclusion must be that building a gatehouse is actually not laudable. What then are we to make of the Mishnah's law?

To clarify the challenge, the Mishnah—the third-century base text upon which the Talmud is commenting and which is considered authoritative by the Talmud—mandates the building of a gatehouse. The Mishnah states this mandate as actionable—one resident might legally coerce a fellow courtyard resident to contribute his portion for the building of the gatehouse. The reasonable conclusion that the Talmud draws from this is that, as a matter of public policy, the building of a gatehouse would seem to be an approved activity. The Talmud challenges this assumption by introducing the story of the prophet Elijah who stopped visiting a certain righteous man as a result of that man's involvement in the building of a gatehouse. This would imply that the building of a gatehouse is *not* an approved or laudable activity. Hence, the problem.

The rhetorical strategy that is followed in these cases is distinguishing between the two instances of seemingly incompatible law. It may seem as if one source claims that a certain activity is forbidden, while the second equally authoritative source claims that that very activity is permitted. However, in truth, the first source only seems to be forbidding the activity, but it is actually only forbidden under certain circumstances.

The Talmud in the continuation of the discussion does just this. It successfully distinguishes between the gatehouse that is discussed in the Mishnah and the gatehouse that the righteous person built, thus preserving both the law of the Mishnah and the correctness of Elijah's posture toward the righteous person. The strategy pursued by the Talmud is to portray the gatehouse of the Mishnah as being more easily entered than that of the righteous person. However, harmonizing this ruling of the Mishnah with the outcome of the Elijah story is not the task that I wish to pursue here.

I am intrigued by another question. How is it or why is it that a story told about Elijah might be able to contradict a Mishnah? The hierarchy of rabbinic literature is dependent on a division into epochs. Mishnah, edited somewhere around the early part of the third century, is the cornerstone of the literature. In order to challenge a ruling found in a Mishnah, one needs to locate a contradictory ruling in another Mishnah or coeval literature such as Tosefta or statements found only in the Talmud but attributed to early sages.[12] While Elijah is a biblical figure, and therefore paradigmatic in certain ways, he is not a legal authority. Why then is this story brought to contradict a Mishnaic ruling?

What, for that matter, did the righteous man do that was so wrong? The Talmud gives us no clue as to his ethical transgression.

Here we turn to the medieval commentators, and in doing so, I will show how the ethic of hearing has informed this legal discussion. The most famous and ubiquitous of the medieval commentators on Talmud is Rabbi Shlomo Yitzhaki (1040–1105), known by his acronym Rashi, who lived in Northern France. Commenting on the phrase "And Elijah no longer spoke with him," Rashi writes, "For it gates off the poor people who are shouting [*tzo'akim*] [for money or assistance] and their voices are not heard." The problem with the gatehouse is that it serves as a buffer to the poor people who might show up to ask for assistance and causes their cries not to be heard. Twice more in this section, Rashi repeats this same claim— the gatehouse is problematic to the extent that the cries of the poor cannot be heard. The word he uses is *tze'akah*, the same word that the Torah uses in Exodus 2:23 and 22:22. The fact that Rashi repeats this comment twice using the very same language underlines its importance to him.

Rashi is not alone in his understanding of the misdeed of the righteous person in the story. There is almost universal agreement among the medieval commentators that this is the problem—the gatehouse will not allow the cry of the poor to be heard. Yet there is no explicit textual clue that would lead Rashi or the others to say this. Rashi (and the commentary tradition which succeeds him) is essentially claiming that this is the obvious answer. The transgression of the righteous person is that his gatehouse would make it impossible to hear the cry of the poor.

This brings us full circle. The "obviousness" of Rashi's understanding is dependent on the understanding of the cry in the Exodus story. The causal relationship between hearing the cry and acting in a just and redemptive way narrated in Exodus 2 and codified in Exodus 23 is what is assumed by Rashi—and pointed to with Rashi's insistent use of the verb *tza'ak*/cry out; hence, the "obviousness" of his interpretation. Hearing the cry paves the way for just action, which leads to redemption. Ignoring the cry leads in the opposite direction.

The story of the *hasid* and Elijah is here to reinforce the point that the seemingly neutral and minor actions of urban planning or house building (such as building a gatehouse) have a much larger context and a larger impact. We can choose to be like Pharaoh and set up our living spaces so that we are never confronted by the demands of the Stranger or by the cries of the poor. Or, by contrast, we can set up our living spaces—our houses, our neighborhoods, and ultimately our cities—so that we are open to the demands of the Stranger. We can choose to act like God and pave the way for redemptive acts of justice. We can choose to act like Pharaoh and refuse to hear.

When we live in urban areas, there are also sometimes real fears and dangers which push us to err on the side of gating ourselves off at the expense of being able to hear the cries of the Stranger. This did not escape the medieval commentators either. In the early twelfth century, the Spanish Rabbi Meir Halevi Abulafiah, a close associate of the royal house, wrote an excursus on our Talmudic text.[13] When faced with the ultimate question: if we set up our urban spaces such that the poor can enter—other, darker, forces can enter too. He said the following:

Yet, here, what benefit is there? And what harm is removed from the courtyard with this gatehouse? For certainly when the poor can enter, so too can thieves enter! Still, this makes no difference.[14]

Still, this makes no difference. There is a more compelling "benefit" to creating a city in which the poor can be heard, than the "harm" of risking burglary. There is a point at which justice must be everyone's priority.

Walking the Talk: Acting Like God or Acting Like Pharaoh

The power of the gatehouse text is that the details and the theoretical principles are inextricably intertwined. There is no moment in which the allegorical or analogical reflex is triggered and we need to say: it's not really about a gatehouse and a courtyard. It *is* really about a gatehouse and a courtyard. The text is about the real actions that people perform and how those concrete actions point toward a larger conceptual framework of justice. Just as each facet of a crystal reflects the entire crystal, so too each action must embody the conception of justice of the whole.

In the text in Baba Bathra, the legitimate action of improving one's property is limited by the need to create the opportunities for strangers and their needs to be present to us. There are legitimate ways to build a gatehouse and illegitimate ways—it all hinges on whether the way we build the gatehouse allows the poor person's cry to be heard. For this is the first step toward just action.

When I make decisions about how I am going to live, those decisions construct a reality which is either just or not. Am I going to live in a gated community? Am I going to live in a community in which I will see indigent or homeless folks on the streets? Am I going to pressure the local police officers to roust the homeless from my neighborhood? Will I oppose the halfway house in my neighborhood or welcome it? Will I be a NIMBY (Not in My Backyard) or a YIMBY (Yes in My Backyard)?[15] When push comes to shove, does my property take precedence over my values?

Once we have entered into this discourse, there is also a larger context for it, a more analogical context perhaps. The larger challenge is figuring out how to pay attention to people who live outside my intimate geography. How do I hear the cries of those I never see and never visit? How do I keep in mind that when I vote on property taxes, the health and education needs of people I will never meet are impacted? How do I retain a focus on the fact that the way I live my life can enhance or endanger the lives of people on the "other side of town"—the other side sometimes being only blocks away?

The rabbinic discussion of the gatehouse suggests that a politics that will create a community of obligation begins with a practice of hearing. Walking on the streets of my neighborhood, I need to see the folks who live on the street as part of my neighborhood. I need to hear them and respond to them. Walking into a supermarket, I should also be thinking of the wages that the stock clerks and the cashiers make; I should see the cashier as part of my neighborhood rather than as part of the cash register. The practice of piety—hearing the cry of the poor—must then lead to a political practice, a practice which causes the city as a whole to engage the larger questions of poverty and homelessness.

The Elijah story is invoked to challenge the law of the Mishnah because the principle at stake is central to the legal tradition—the notion that one must be able to hear the cry of the poor. If one can hear the cry, one can choose to be like God. Precluding the possibility of hearing the cry of the poor is itself a choice—a choice to be like Pharaoh.

Notes

1 "Posterity," in *Overlord: Poems* (Harper Collins Publishers, 2005), 86.

2 http://www.loc.gov/exhibits/religion/f0402as.jpg (accessed June 22, 2009, 11:46 a.m.).

3 An article in *Harper's New Monthly Magazine*, July 1856, by Ben Lossing (p. 180) confirms that this was indeed intended as a design for the Great Seal.

4 Many a wag has pointed out that the second part of the verse, "So that they shall worship Me," was not part of our slogan.

5 Cf., for example, Obery Hendricks, *The Politics of Jesus: Rediscovering the True Revolutionary Nature of Jesus' Teachings and How They Have Been Corrupted* (Doubleday, 2006) as one recent example of this frequently argued meaning of the Exodus.

6 This is explicitly so. See Exodus 13:14, "And when, in time to come, your son asks you, saying, 'What does this mean?' you shall say to him, 'It was with a mighty hand that the LORD brought us out from Egypt, the house of bondage."

7 See note 5 above. This understanding is also present in the medieval commentary tradition. See the commentary of *Rashbam* (Rabbenu Shlomo ben Meir) (the French commentator who wrote in the twelfth century) on Exodus 22:20 on the phrase, "for you were aliens in Egypt": "As it is explained before us 'and you know the soul of the stranger for you were strangers.' (Exod. 23:9) Since his pain is great, so too is the punishment [for his pain]." For a contemporary example from a writer in the Jewish tradition, see this column on the weekly Torah portion in the popular secular Israeli newspaper *Yediot Aharanot*: "Have we forgotten the covenant which created the Jewish religion? 'Do not oppress the stranger for you were strangers in the land of Egypt.' Have we forgotten the sacred alchemy of turning suffering into compassion?" (http://www.ynetnews.com/articles/0,7340,L-3203786,00.html. accessed 10/04/10 at 12:35 p.m.)

8 Defining what exactly Mishnah is—whether code or casebook or textbook— is the subject of scholarly debate. For a recent article which summarizes the state of the debate, see Yaakov Elman, "Order, Sequence, and Selection: The Mishnah's Anthological Choices," in David Stern, ed. *The Anthology in Jewish Literature* (Oxford University Press, 2004), 53–80.

9 "Commentary" is both an apt and a completely inapt description of the Talmud. For a recent and current introductory discussion of some of the issues, see Lawrence Shiffman, "The Making of the Mishnah and the Talmud," and Yaakov Ellman, "The Babylonian Talmud in Its Historical Context," both in Sharon Lieberman Mintz and Gabriel M. Goldstein, *Printing the Talmud: From Bomberg to Schottenstein* (Yeshiva University Museum, 2005).

10 Originally, Nezikin was one tractate. It was subsequently divided into three parts or "gates."

¹¹ In the service of brevity and clarity, I have personified "the Talmud" and, in so doing, have sacrificed some scholarly accuracy. For the most part, when I write "the Talmud" in this essay, I intend the anonymous editorial layer referred to as the *stam*. For the fundamental role of the *stam* in the shaping of the Babylonian Talmud, see Jeffrey Rubenstein, *The Culture of the Babylonian Talmud* (Johns Hopkins University Press, 2003).

¹² This epochal division is found in the Talmud itself—noted in the breach. See B Ketubot 8a where the *stam* questions how Rav, an amora, a Talmudic sage, can challenge a law found in the Mishnah. The answer is that Rav is considered as a Tanna.

¹³ On Abulafiah, see Bernard Septimus, *Hispano-Jewish Culture in Transition: The Career and Controversies of Ramah* (Harvard University Press, 1982).

¹⁴ *Sefer Yad Ramah*, (Heb.) (n.d.) folio 13, p. 25.

¹⁵ Not in my backyard or yes in my backyard.

Chapter 2

The Obligation of Protest

So much seems to depend upon a cow, a very specific cow; Rabbi Elazar's cow to be exact. It is a cow which defied the sages, and the sages were not happy.

> Rabbi Elazar ben Azaryah's cow would go out with a strap between its horns against the will of the sages. (Mishnah Shabbat, 5:4)[1]

Now, admittedly, this pronouncement follows an anonymous—and therefore, at least rhetorically, unanimous—law which explicitly stated, "And a cow . . . should not [go out on Shabbat] with a strap between its horns." Immediately, it appears, Rabbi Elazar's cow flew in the face of this rabbinic ruling and walked out (presumably of its pen/Rabbi Elazar's house/barn, etc.) into the public domain flaunting its horn strap.[2]

The striking thing about this is that the agency is ascribed to the cow. The Mishnah does not relate that Rabbi Elazar ben Azaryah *allowed* his cow to go out; or that Rabbi Elazar ben Azaryah urged his cow to go out; or that Rabbi Elazar ben Azaryah—in order to make his point that he thought the rest of the sages were dead wrong on this issue—paraded his cow in Bet She'arim Square adorned with her Shabbat horn strap.

On the other hand, the cow is known to us only as Rabbi Elazar ben Azaryah's cow. This again is an odd way to go about having a Mishnaic dispute. One would have expected something on the order of "Rabbi Elazar ben Azaryah said, 'The cow may go out on the Shabbat with a strap between its horns.'" It's almost as if the cow story is cited as a sage story might be—so that we may learn from it.

The two Talmuds differ in their approach to this bit of text. The sixth-century Palestinian Talmud treats this line *as if* it had actually been an argument, as if it had read, "Rabbi Elazar ben Azaryah said, 'The cow may go out on the Shabbat with a strap between its horns.'" It then introduces a dispute about the meaning of this dispute. This manner of interpretation is pretty standard when there is an actual dispute. The legal logic would then demand that the dispute be clarified: what is the reasoning behind the fact that Rabbi Elazar ben Azaryah disagrees with everybody else?[3]

The Babylonian Talmud goes in a completely different direction. It seems that the BT is also stuck on the oddness of the phrase, "Rabbi Elazar ben Azaryah's cow." Perhaps it too is bothered by the fact that the action is ascribed to the cow. In any event, for the BT, naming the cow after Rabbi Elazar ben Azaryah is a reason to reflect and a cause to question.

To the Bavli's ear, the Mishnah's statement sounds as if Rabbi Elazar ben Azaryah had only one cow. ("Rabbi Elazar ben Azaryah's cow . . .") However, the editors of the Babylonian Talmud seem to have known that Rabbi Elazar ben Azaryah had far more than the one cow. They cite a tradition attributed to Rav (a third-century CE Babylonian sage or amora) which credited Rabbi Elazar ben Azaryah with tithing twelve thousand lambs every year.[4] Doing the math, this brings the entire herd to at least one hundred and twenty thousand animals a year. What then is meant by the quaint description, "Rabbi Elazar ben Azaryah's cow"?

The answer proffered by the Talmud is that the cow actually belonged to Rabbi Elazar ben Azaryah's neighbor. However, since Rabbi Elazar ben Azaryah did not protest the fact that his neighbor let her cow out with a strap between its horns, the cow and its actions were ascribed to Rabbi Elazar ben Azaryah—and it was Rabbi Elazar ben Azaryah with whom the sages were displeased.[5]

This resolves two problems. The dispute in the Mishnah which does not look like a dispute—or is not written in a dispute form—is not actually a dispute. Rabbi Elazar ben Azaryah actually agrees with everybody else that horn straps are forbidden for cows on the Sabbath. Rabbi Elazar ben Azaryah aroused the ire of the sages only because he did not lodge a protest with his neighbor when she let her cow flaunt her horn strap in public, or make an attempt to stop her. Rabbi Elazar ben Azaryah was guilty of not intervening when a transgression occurred. Therefore, the cow and its deed are attributed to Rabbi Elazar ben Azaryah even though he obviously had many, many cows—and this cow was not actually one of those cows. One other reason for the Bavli's insistence that "the cow belonging to Rabbi Elazar" denotes far more than "Rabbi Elazar's cow" might be that the Mishnah records Rabbi Elazar saying it is *permitted* for a cow to go out with a horn strap on the Sabbath. (Mishnah Beitzah 2:7) This being established as his opinion, the editors of BT might have said, why would this dispute not be rehearsed here? Why would the Mishnah be articulated in such a cryptic manner?

"Rabbi Elazar's cow" becomes shorthand for "one who had the opportunity to protest against a wrongdoing but did not." This then—the protest or lack thereof—is the frame for, and becomes the theme of the discussion.

Before continuing, we ought to articulate the most troublesome part of the explanation that the cow actually belonged to the neighbor. Why is Rabbi Elazar ben Azaryah responsible? What is he responsible for? Is he obligated to make sure that no profanation of the Shabbat happens? Or is he obligated to make sure that no one profanes the Shabbat? Is his obligation toward God (no desecration should happen) or toward people (no one should desecrate)? This will be an important question to answer if we want to extrapolate from this principle a more universal principle of action—especially in a case when there is third-party involvement. That is, in a case where the wrong action was not that a cow wandered about with a strap between its horns, but was rather that a person was harming another. In that case, what is my responsibility? Am I obligated to the injured party to prevent the injury? Or am I obligated to God that no injury should be done? It could also be that in this, I am obligated to save the transgressor from committing an injury or a sin.[6]

The discussion that is generated in the Talmud on the heels of this new understanding of Rabbi Elazar ben Azaryah's (neighbor's) cow leads us to a consideration of one's obligation to stop bad actors from acting badly anywhere that action happens. The anonymity of the neighbor, and other actors in the text, reinforces the idea that my responsibility is also to people whose names I do not know, and I am obligated to prevent injustice being perpetrated by people I don't know.[7] As I am reading this text, its claim is that I have an obligation to prevent wrong or injustice from happening to, or being done by, anybody. Cashing out this obligation is the work of political practice.

We have, however, gotten ahead of ourselves.

In order to get from here to there, we will pass through three textual moments. The first is a statement of law, the second is a profoundly disturbing story of sages acting badly (and other sages calling them on it), and the third moment is a rereading of a powerful prophetic moment from the book of Ezekiel.

I. The Law

The Talmudic discussion continues from the statement of Rabbi Elazar ben Azaryah's responsibility:[8]

> Rav, R. Hanina, R. Yohanan, and R. Haviva taught, [. . .]
> All who can protest against [something wrong that] one of their family [is doing] and does not protest, is accountable[9] together with their family.
> [All who can protest against something wrong that] a citizen of their city [is doing and does not protest], is accountable together with all citizens of the city.
> [All who can protest against something wrong that is being done] in the whole world, is accountable together with all citizens of the world.

What is meant here by "protest"? This word—*machah* in Hebrew in the verb form; *mecha'ah* is the Hebrew noun[10]—has a pretty stable field of meaning in rabbinic literature. It usually means verbally demanding that another stop doing something. The activities that are or could be (or are not able to be) protested against in rabbinic literature range from the profane (noise coming from a shop,[11] moving a window a hand's breadth[12]) to the sacred (saying the explicit name of God).[13] The principle of this statement is that not protesting against an action comes close to supporting that action—close enough to be considered as if one is doing the action.

Another important term here is "can." Does "can" mean the physical ability to protest (as is the case in other instances where face-to-face protest is required)? Or does it mean that there is a real possibility that the protest might be listened to?

Rashi (Rabbi Shlomo Yitzhaki), the eleventh- to twelfth-century commentator from Northern France, understands that "can protest" means that one's protest has the possibility to be effective. In commenting on the last line that we quoted above ("in the whole world"), Rashi writes that this refers to "a king or a patriarch who has the ability to protest for people are afraid of them and fulfill their decrees."[14] Rashi, of course, is writing in the context of a feudal state in the twelfth century. It is important to think of what the implications would be for a democracy, where seemingly it is the citizens whose decrees must be fulfilled.

On the other hand, Rabbi Menahem HaMeiri, who lived in Provence in the thirteenth and fourteenth centuries, drew a different conclusion from these texts. He wrote, "The king is punished for the sin of the nation because he did not protest against them; and the nation as a whole is punished for the sin of the king because they did not protest against him." One need not *be* the king to protest.

A question that we will encounter further on in the text is whether protest is important in and of itself or whether there is a need for a plausible chance of success in order to be obligated to protest. If protest is an individual's obligation, even in a situation where there is no chance of impacting the injustice being protested against, the act of protest, then, is about preserving one's own "purity." If one did not protest, one had not made clear that one stood outside the cultural or societal boundaries of injustice.

If, however, protest is an obligation only when there is a plausible chance of success, the act of protest is then an act which need only be performed when one can change some unwanted outcome for the better.

For now, we can understand the opening part of the Talmud's discussion as setting out the circles of responsibility. This part concludes with the following lines:

> Said R. Papa: "These of the house of the Exilarch are punished for all the world."
> R. Hanina said:[15] "Why is it written: 'The LORD will enter into judgment with the elders of His people, and the princes thereof" (Isa. 3:14). If the princes sinned, what did the elders do?
> Rather, say that the elders did not protest against the princes."

Rav Papa's[16] statement serves to reduce the applicability of the obligation to protest against a wrong done anywhere in the world. He seems to be saying that it is only the exilarch and his court—the political leadership of the Jewish community in Babylonia—who are "punished" for wrongdoing anywhere in the world. This would seem to be a result of the fact that they have the ability to make effective protest.

Rav Hanina, on the other hand, cites a prooftext to support the contention that despite not having "real" political power, the sages are held responsible for the actions of the political leadership. The "prooftext" is actually a verse that is interpreted by the biblical hermeneutic principles employed by the sages.[17] In its context, the verse is part of a longer prophecy in which Isaiah is channeling God's rage about the injustices to the poor that the leadership of the people have perpetrated. God is going to make things right. While Isaiah does not distinguish between "elders" and "princes," using the two terms synonymously, Rav Hanina does. Rav Hanina interprets elders as "the sages" (echoing the "seventy elders" who accompanied Moses to the foot of Mount Sinai),[18] and "the princes" as the political leadership. Therefore, Rav Hanina wonders, why would God punish the sages? The sages "obviously" did not steal from the poor (as the continuation of the verse in Isaiah claims). It was obviously the princes who did that. Rav Hanina's point, however, is that the sages share culpability because they did not protest the acts of the princes. Relative powerlessness is not an excuse for the rabbis.

The basic point remains. One has a responsibility to stop an act that is happening in the spheres of one's existence—which spheres reach out to the world. East Los Angeles is part of my world, as is Jerusalem, as is Darfur, in the Sudan. This does not speak to the question of hierarchy but rather to the basic question of responsibility. The question of responsibility does also impact the question of hierarchy or priority.[19]

There are of course many questions that are left open. What qualifies as a protest? How long must one protest? By what means should one protest? Are there any means that are disqualified? Violence? Shaming? Is protest the same thing as bringing something to an end? And so on.

The obvious next step in this discussion would be for the Talmud to start dealing with these questions. In a sense, it does that.

II. The Story

As is the practice of the Talmud, a story is introduced at this point. I will cite the whole story and then review it line by line.

> R. Yehudah was sitting in front of [i.e., was learning from] Shmuel.
> A certain woman came.
> She cried out before him and he paid no attention.
> He [R. Yehudah] said to him: "Does the Master not hold that 'One Who stops his ears at the cry of the poor, he also shall cry himself, but shall not be answered?'" (Prov. 21:13).
> He [Shmuel] said to him: "Sharp one! Your head [i.e., Shmuel] is cold. Your head's head is in the heat!
> Mar Uqba is sitting as the head of the court."
> For it is written: O house of David, thus said the LORD: Execute justice in the morning, and deliver the spoiled out of the hand of the oppressor, lest My fury go forth like fire, and burn that none can quench it, because of the evil of your doings (Jer. 21:12).

The story is set in the most natural of all situations for the sages: a younger sage is learning from a senior sage. The identity of the sages is instructive. Shmuel, a second-century sage, was with Rav, the founder of the academies in Babylonia; that is, he was the "father" of Rabbinic Judaism in Babylonia. This is to make the point that he is not your run-of-the-mill rabbi. He is an important sage. Rav Yehudah was no slouch either. Though the junior member at this time, he is credited with creating a third academy at Pumbeditha after his training with both Shmuel and Rav.

Rav Yehudah then was literally "sitting in front of" Shmuel, which might denote the actual pedagogical scene, and definitely the difference in their status.[20] Until rather late in the history of the rabbinic enterprise in Babylonia, there were no brick-and-mortar academies. A student would therefore just sit in front of a master either inside a house or outside under a tree.[21] This is somewhat important as it makes the sages accessible to passersby. Scene two involves a passerby.

As they are studying, a woman approaches. We are told nothing about her except that she approaches. We are then told that she is crying out or shouting to them for help. Her cries are ignored.

Rav Yehudah, it seems, was looking to his teacher to react in some way. No reaction was forthcoming. Finally, Rav Yehudah rebuked his teacher. His rebuke seems to articulate in one sentence the principle that we defined in chapter 1—the obligation to listen to the cry of the Stranger. Rav Yehudah asks Shmuel pointedly if he, Shmuel, does not abide by the teaching of Proverbs which makes the strong claim that if one does not hear the cry of the poor, then one's own cries will go unanswered.

Rav Yehudah seems to be rightly saying to Shmuel: "How can you ignore this woman and continue to teach Torah? Is this not a fundamental principle of Torah—to choose to act like God and not Pharaoh?"

Shmuel's answer is less than satisfactory. He parries Rav Yehudah's demand by saying that since he—Shmuel—is not the political leader, since he does not have official authority, he has no culpability. It is Mar Uqba who is culpable. Finally, as a coup de grace, Shmuel cites Jeremiah 21:12 as a prooftext. However, instead of raising up the demand to "execute justice . . . .and deliver the spoiled out of the hand of the oppressor," Shmuel finds in this verse a reason to ignore a woman's cry. Shmuel reads the opening words of the verse very strictly: "O house of David. . . ." That is, according to Shmuel's interpretation, *only* the House of David is culpable. He has nothing to worry about.

While Shmuel's role in the story is disturbing, the woman's role is perplexing. On the one hand, there is something of a subgenre of "women crying out" stories. The structure of those stories is all the same: an unnamed woman comes to a number of sages and cries out about something; the senior sage among them ignores her.[22] It is not therefore surprising within the literary boundaries of the Babylonian Talmud that the woman is ignored. The difference between all the other stories and this one is that here, we never find out what the woman was distressed about. It seems that this story is about the very idea of crying out and (not) answering. Again, this is the issue that we limned in chapter 1 in our discussion of the gatehouse and the *hasid* in Baba Bathra 7b. The woman, in her literary role,[23] is the poor person. She is the marginal Other.

Shmuel is a somewhat more fleshed-out character here— within the limitations of Talmudic storytelling. The "sage who ignores" plays a central supporting role in one of the so-called legends of the destruction of the Temple. One of the collections of these legends is found in Tractate Gittin of the Babylonian Talmud (55b). The story which will flesh out the meaning of the sage who ignores is referred to by the Talmud as "Kamtza and Bar Kamtza." The Talmud introduces this tale with the tag line: "On account of Kamtza and Bar Kamtza Jerusalem was destroyed."[24]

This tale unfolds as a story of mistaken identity. Kamtza and Bar Kamtza are names. Names that, obviously, are easily mistaken. There was, according to the story, an important man who is unnamed, who was friendly with Kamtza and an enemy of Bar Kamtza. He threw a party and had his servant invite everybody who was anybody—including Kamtza but, of course, not Bar Kamtza. The man's servant, however, mistakenly invited Bar Kamtza instead of Kamtza. At the party, when the host saw that Bar Kamtza was there (was the party thrown in order to exclude Bar Kamtza?), he was enraged. He demanded that Bar Kamtza immediately leave. Bar Kamtza, in trying to avoid the public humiliation of being kicked out of the party, offered to pay for his food. Then he offered to pay for half the party. Finally, he offered to pay for the whole party. The host was adamant and physically removed Bar Kamtza.

Bar Kamtza looked around and saw that all the sages were present, and none of them had raised a finger to help him out. He thought to himself: "Since they did not protest,[25] they must agree with what is happening." In his anger at his public humiliation—and the fact that the sages did not rise to his defense—he hatched a plot to convince the caesar that the Jews were rebelling. The plot succeeded and the caesar destroyed Jerusalem. The relevant point of the story is that the sages did not respond to Bar Kamtza's humiliation and caused the destruction of the Temple. Shmuel did exactly as the sages of the Kamtza-Bar Kamtza story did, except that he articulated a justification for his ignoring the woman.

One might be tempted to ask: What is this story doing here? It is not a story about (not) protesting; it is a story about (not) aiding. This perhaps is a clue to its purpose. The story is not only about Shmuel's inaction but about Rav Yehudah's action. Whereas the statement immediately prior to the story (Rav Hanina's statement) argues for the culpability of both sages and princes, not excusing those without official authority, Shmuel's statements seem to directly contradict that. However, Rav Yehudah's actions—protesting to his teacher about his teacher's (in)action—follow directly from the logic of Rav Hanina's midrash. Rav Yehudah is not constrained by the power of the hierarchy when given the opportunity to act. Shmuel is.

This story disturbed even its earliest readers. The following comment is preserved in the fourteenth-century collection of Tosafot commentaries to Tractate Baba Bathra. The comment itself is attributed to the eleventh-century North African sage Rabbenu Hananel:

> The Gaonim [i.e., the heads of the Academies in Babylonia from after the close of the Talmud, approximately the seventh century CE] report that they have a tradition handed down from teacher to teacher that the phrase "upside down world" refers to seeing Shmuel [in Heaven] sitting in front of [i.e., studying from] Rav Yehudah his student. This is because Rav

Yehudah protested against Shmuel in the story in Shabbat 55a
(*Tosafot s.v. 'elyonim lema'alah vetahtonim lematah*, Baba Bathra
10b).

This statement directly comments on an "out of body experience"
had by one of the sages who was very sick and almost died. When
asked by his father, "What did you see?" he answered, "I saw an
upside-down world." He doesn't explain his statement any further.
His father replies, "You saw the true world." The tradition that
was transmitted shortly after the text was composed connects this
statement with our story of Shmuel and Rav Yehudah. The "upside-
down world" was the one in which the teacher, Shmuel, sits in
front of his student Rav Yehudah. This, however, is the true world,
because Rav Yehudah was the one who protested while Shmuel
was silent.

    This midrashic reading of the statement in Baba Bathra 10b
as a way of interpreting our story supports our discomfort with
the story and our reading of Rav Yehudah's role in the narrative.
Shmuel seems to understand that he has an obligation to act justly,
not an obligation to make sure justice happens and injustice is
thwarted. Therefore, if he is not himself the bad actor, he has
fulfilled his obligation. In the interaction with the woman, he has
decided that the appropriate actor is the exilarch; therefore, it is not
even incumbent upon him to find out the particulars of the woman's
story. Rav Yehudah, along with the tradition, seems to take the
opposite stance. There is an obligation to ensure that justice happens
and injustice is thwarted. One must listen to and hear the cry of the
oppressed—and then be claimed by it and act accordingly. It is Rav
Yehudah whom we raise up.

III. The Prophetic Moment

The sugya continues,
R. Zera[26] said to R. Simon: "The Master should rebuke these
of the house of the partriarch."
He [R. Simon] said to him: "They will not accept [the rebuke]
from me."
He said to him: "Even though they will not accept it, the
Master should rebuke them."

This exchange opens with R. Zera challenging or urging R. Simon to rebuke the political leadership. The reason for the rebuke is left unstated. We have no way of knowing if the matter was one of ritual or whether there was some civil injustice that was being perpetrated. R. Simon obviously knows what R. Zera is referring to. His reply is that a rebuke would be unwarranted since it will fall on deaf ears. R. Zera replies that this should not be a deciding factor.

What is the discussion about?

First, R. Zera, following Rav Yehudah's lead[27] urges that protests should be lodged against the political authority. His basic stance is that nobody is exempt from protest. His second point (after R. Simon's demurral) is a point about protest itself. This point can be understood in one of two ways. Either R. Zera is urging an agnostic stance toward the political leadership. That is, until you are sure that they will not listen to you, you must rebuke them. Or R. Zera is making a much more far-reaching point about protest itself. There is an obligation to protest or rebuke independent of the efficacy of any specific act of protest. The obligation then, is not connected to the ability to stop the activity. This latter type of protest is more in line with the Christian notion of "witness." The protest is an act which defines the line between good and evil, even if it ultimately fails in stopping the evil.

The rest of the sugya places this discussion in stark mythic terms, rereading a prophecy from the book of Ezekiel in which the righteous of Jerusalem are slain by God together with the iniquitous, because the righteous did not protest the iniquity.

Before proceeding, I would like to tarry briefly at this moment. R. Zera's advocacy for activism stands on its own. He seems to be saying that if injustice is being perpetrated in the world, the only way to be just is to stand against that injustice. This is not to argue for a utopian political practice, rather it is an argument against a political practice which gives utility not only a vote but a veto. At times, all we can do to practice our humanity is to say, "We are not complicit in this action." If we always allow ourselves to fall victim to the seeming futility of justice, injustice will inevitably prevail, and the image of God which we each carry in the form of doing justice will inevitably lose more and more of its luster.

R. Zera brings support for his contention from a tradition attributed to R. Aha, son of R. Hanina, who taught,

> Never did a good decree leave the mouth of the Holy One of Blessing which then [the Holy One of Blessing] turned to evil except concerning this matter.
> For it is written: And God said to him, pass through the city, through Jerusalem, and make a mark on the foreheads of the men who are sighing and groaning for all the abominations that have been done in it [Jerusalem] (Ezek. 9:4).

R. Aha's claim in its starkest version is that the only thing that ever motivated God to change a good decree into a bad one was the lack of protest in a situation which warranted it. As this text unfolds, we will see that R. Aha is referring to God punishing righteous people because they did not protest against the actions of others.

The story that R. Aha is referring to is found in Ezekiel chapter 9. Ezekiel, in a prophetic trance, is transported to the city of Jerusalem, where he is led on a tour of the abominations that the people of Judah have committed—including "seventy men, elders of the House of Israel" (8:12). God promises Ezekiel that retribution is on the way. "I in turn will act with fury, I will show no pity or compassion; though they cry aloud to Me, I will not listen to them," God says at the close of chapter 8. Chapter 9 is the tale of that retribution. I will quote it in full since the artistry of the midrashist, the rabbinic interpreter, becomes apparent only on the background of the original story—the literal or contextual meaning.

Ezekiel 9

1 Then He called loudly in my hearing, saying, "Approach, you men in charge of the city, each bearing his weapons of destruction!"
2 And six men entered by way of the upper gate that faces north, each with his club in his hand; and among them was another, clothed in linen, with a writing case at his waist. They came forward and stopped at the bronze altar.
3 Now the Presence of the God of Israel had moved from the cherub on which it had rested to the platform of the

House. He called to the man clothed in linen with the writing case at his waist;

4 and the LORD said to him, "Pass through the city, through Jerusalem, and put a mark on the foreheads of the men who moan and groan because of all the abominations that are committed in it."

5 To the others He said in my hearing, "Follow him through the city and strike; show no pity or compassion.

6 Kill off graybeard, youth and maiden, women and children; but do not touch any person who bears the mark. Begin here at My Sanctuary." So they began with the elders who were in front of the House.

7 And He said to them, "Defile the House and fill the courts with the slain. Then go forth." So they went forth and began to kill in the city.

8 When they were out killing, and I remained alone, I flung myself on my face and cried out, "Ah, Lord GOD! Are you going to annihilate all that is left of Israel, pouring out Your fury upon Jerusalem?"

9 He answered me, "The iniquity of the Houses of Judah and Israel is very very great, the land is full of crime and the city is full of corruption. For they say, 'The LORD has forsaken the land, and the LORD does not see.'

10 I, in turn, will show no pity or compassion; I will give them their deserts."

11 And then the man clothed in linen with the writing case at his waist brought back word, saying, "I have done as You commanded me."

In the original story in Ezekiel, God wreaks vengeance upon the evil and saves the righteous. God spares the victims[28] of the abominations and has everyone else killed. To Ezekiel's protest: "Are you going to annihilate all that is left of Israel, pouring out Your fury upon Jerusalem?" God's answer is, "I . . . will show no pity or compassion; I will give them their deserts."

This chilling vision is reconstructed by the deft reading of R. Aha. He starts with verse 4, answering the question who gets marked and why. R. Aha invents a conversation between God and the angel Gavriel (apparently "the man clothed in linen with the writing case at his waist" of the previous verse).

Said the Holy One of Blessing to Gavriel:
"Go and write on the foreheads of the righteous an ink mark
so that the angels of destruction will not have power over
them.
And on the foreheads of the wicked a mark of blood so that
the angels of destruction shall have power over them."

This is not much more than is written in Ezekiel, except that those who moaned and groaned because of the abomination are now labeled righteous and the others are wicked. It is this second mark which is new. It also prompts "Truth" to intervene before Gavriel has a chance to act.

Truth said to the Holy One of Blessing: "Master of the World,
how are these different than these?"
God said to her: "These are completely righteous and these
are completely wicked."
She said before God: "Master of the World, they were able to
protest and they did not protest."
God said to her: "It is revealed and known to me that if they
had protested, they would not have accepted the protest."
She said to God: "Master of the World, though it is revealed
to You, is it revealed to them?"

Truth speaks the voice of reality to God's binary world of good and evil. There is culpability enough to spread around. Truth's winning argument is that even though God might know that the protests of the righteous would have fallen on deaf ears, the righteous could not have been sure of that. Since this is so, they had an obligation to protest against the acts of the wicked. Not having protested places them in the same category as those who committed the acts.

This conversation took place between verses 4 and 5. God, in verse 5 and especially verse 6 gives the divine minions their marching orders.

This is what is written: An old man, a young man, a maiden, children, women, wipe them out completely. But all
who have the mark do not touch; and start with my Temple
(Ezek. 9:6).

And it also is written: And they started with the elders in front of the House (Ezek. 9:6).

Why start with the elders in front of the House? There seem to be two midrashic readings here. First, the identification of "elders" with righteous ("old in wisdom" as the Talmudic saying goes). Second, the term "my Temple" is reread.

R. Yosef taught: "Do not read 'my temple' (*mikdashi*), but rather, 'my sanctified ones' (*mekudashay*). These are people who fulfilled the Torah from Aleph to Tav."
And immediately: And here, six people approach from the Upper Gate which faces north, and each person has their tool of destruction in their hand, and amongst them is one dressed in linens and the scribe's case is by his side. And they approached and stood beside the bronze altar (Ezek. 9:2).

God, after the conversation with Truth, ordered that the killing start with "my sanctified ones." It is only then that the mission begins—reading verse 2 *after* verse 6. Only after Truth's clarification is it clear who gets the sign—only one who was righteous and protested against wickedness.

Returning to R. Zera, his argument with R. Simon is that only God can know that a protest is futile. From the point of view of mere mortals, the obligation to protest is absolute.

Conclusion

There are three moments in the Talmud's discussion of the obligation to protest. The relationship between them is not the linear continuity of a narrative nor the question and answer of a Socratic dialogue. The first moment is the introduction of a law—a law without explanation. This does not imply that the law is irrational, only that, as we might expect in contemporary legal codes, the law is introduced as binding and is left unexplained. Just as we are settling in to this moment of pure prescription, a grounding is introduced for one of the laws. This grounding is a certain reading of a verse from the Torah, a claim that the verse from the Torah leads to the law. It is an open question whether this supplies an *explanation* for the law or whether it is only a *grounding* of the law—that is, an authoritative source which would move one to acquiesce in the understanding that this law is binding.

The law that is introduced in this first moment is also a demand of justice: one has an obligation to take responsibility for the actions that are committed in one's circles of existence—one's family, one's city, and the world. The mode of taking responsibility for the actions is an obligation to intervene to stop bad or wicked actions.

The second moment is a narrative moment. A *ma'aseh*, or a story with heuristic significance, is told. The story seems to contradict the basic premise of everything that was just introduced in the first moment of the text. The central character, an important sage, refuses to take responsibility for a woman who cries out for his help.

The third moment is almost completely midrash. An exchange between two scholars generates a midrashic reading of a prophetic vision from the book and the prophet Ezekiel. The midrashic reading makes the strong claim that one is obligated to protest against wicked deeds even when there is no chance of the protest being successful in changing the behavior. The claim comes in the form of a dispute between God and *middat ha-din* which is something like a divine personification of the demands of a strict justice without compassion. *Middat ha-din* appears several times in the Babylonian Talmud to challenge God on a point of justice, always pushing God away from compassion to strict fairness—which leads to someone getting punished.

How is one to understand these moments? The move from the first moment to the second is baffling. Where one is expecting a story which supports the general line of the law which preceded, the reader actually is moved, shoved perhaps, to the other side of the spectrum. A respected sage, one of the founders of the academies in Babylonia, refuses to take responsibility for attempting to assuage a woman's pain, to even hear the woman's cry.

Similarly, the move from the second moment to the third is equally jarring. Following this story of rabbinic indifference comes the absolute demand to protest, even in a situation in which the protest will bear no fruit.

Is there then a bottom line to this discussion? I want to suggest that the intuition which was inscribed as "a teaching passed down from teacher to teacher from the days of the Geonim" is correct. This intuition calls for a reading of the second moment based on the first and the third moments of the texts. Another way of saying this is that the reader's rereading of the second moment (the story of Shmuel, the woman who cried for help and Rav Yehudah) is determined by her knowing the other two moments. If we wanted to smooth out the many bumps and twists in this textual progression, we could state the following.

As a principle of justice, one is obligated to endeavor to intervene when an injustice is happening in an attempt to stop that injustice. However, the actual ability to stop the injustice does not determine the obligation to intervene.

The narrative in the middle of this text is then a cautionary tale in which hierarchy is pitted against justice. The story warns against becoming complacent in one's own status at the expense of constant vigilance in the service of justice. Rav Yehudah would be our example and not Shmuel. Rav Yehudah ignored his standing relative to Shmuel in order to try to force Shmuel to intervene. Shmuel seems to have elevated status above justice.

Turning back to the beginning of this text, we are reminded that the discussion in the Bavli was born of the Mishnaic statement about Rabbi Elazar's cow. I would like to raise up the fact that, when we accept the Bavli's reading, the owner of the cow, Rabbi Elazar ben Azaryah's neighbor is not named. Neither is the woman who cries out to Shmuel. The concentric circles of responsibility legislated in the text attributed to Rav, R. Hanina, R. Yohanan, and R. Haviva also move from the intimate to the anonymous—things that are happening somewhere in the world to people I know of but do not know. This is the crux of the problem of protest. This is the community that an ethic of protest (ultimately an ethic of responsibility) might build.

From Ancient Greece and on, there was always an ethic of intimacy, an ethic based on hospitality. The hearth was sacred. If someone was brought within your home, you were responsible for them. The ethical challenge was always posed by those you did not know. Biblically, this was the failure of the residents of Sodom and Gomorrah in Genesis and of the residents of Gibeah (Judg. 19) who refused to allow one of their intimates to afford hospitality to an outsider. This type of ethic of intimacy runs the serious risk of being generous to those one knows while erecting impermeable boundaries against the Stranger.

I want to suggest that the work that the Talmud is doing here is claiming that interactions with anonymous others must be sites of justice — that the obligation to justice does not stem from an ethic of intimacy, but rather from the absolute responsibility of each person for justice in the world. Emmanuel Levinas, in describing his philosophical project, writes, "Concretely our effort consists in maintaining, within anonymous community, the society of the I with the Other. . . ." This, I want to suggest, is the claim of our text. The claim is that I have an obligation to prevent wrong or injustice from happening to, or being done by, anybody. My obligation is not only to "those in my household." My obligation stretches beyond to those with whom I am in an anonymous community — those whom I do not know. This web of anonymous relationships is constitutive of society in our cities. This ethic of obligation is the way toward making those relationships sites of justice.

Notes

¹ The full text of the *sugya* (Talmudic discussion) is in the appendix to this chapter, page 62 below.

² In general, Mishnah Shabbat chapter 5 details those things with which one's animal is allowed to wander around outside a pen on the Sabbath. This discussion is something of a second-order discussion about "carrying" on Shabbat. "Carrying" is forbidden. It is one of the forty-nine categories of forbidden work which the Mishnah lists in chapter 7 of Mishnah Shabbat. "Carrying" is defined (loosely, as there are many pages of details) as bringing something from a private to a public domain or vice versa, or transporting an object more than four cubits (something around seventy-two inches) within a public domain. Much of Tractate Shabbat is taken up with defining all of these terms: What is "public?" What is "private?" What is an "object?" What is "transporting?" What is a "domain?" and so on.

³ The Palestinian Talmud does eventually get to the idea that Rabbi Elazar's cow might not actually be his. The Talmud then proposes one of two possibilities: either it is his wife's or his neighbors'.

⁴ There is some doubt raised about the veracity of this source by Rabbi Yaakov of Troyes, known as Rabbenu Tam, the twelfth-century Talmud scholar who founded the style and school of the Tosafists. He points out that according to Talmudic sources, Rabbi Elazar ben Azaryah would have been no more than fifteen when the Temple was destroyed. Further, there was no tithing of animals after the destruction of the Temple. It is then not very plausible that Rabbi Elazar ben Azaryah actually tithed twelve thousand animals (Tosafot to Shabbat 54b *s.v. hava me'aser;* cf. Tosafot to Yoma 66a *s.v. ein makdishin*).

⁵ This bit of creative interpretation trails the Mishnah itself by several centuries. The tradition about Rabbi Elazar ben Azaryah cannot be later than the early third century CE (the date of the editing of the Mishnah). The Talmud's interpretation comes from the anonymous editorial voice which is not earlier than the sixth or seventh century CE. There are other Talmudic sources that seem to testify to Rabbi Elazar ben Azaryah's wealth. Aside from the source attributed here to Rav, there is also an anonymous statement in Tractate Kiddushin that implies that Rabbi Elazar ben Azaryah had great wealth.

⁶ This would be the view resulting from an analysis of the interesting law of *rodef*—the preemptive killing of one who seemingly is about to commit a murder or worship idols. One of the reasons given for the decision that the *rodef*/the pursuer should be killed is that "we save the person from the sin with that person's own life." This is some form of killing the person to save his soul (Tosafot to Bavli Sanhedrin 73a *s.v. lehatzilo benafsho*).

⁷ The special prosecutor of the International Criminal Court charged with investigating the genocide in Darfur has said that genocide is characterized by evil being perpetrated by bureaucrats. The anonymity of the perpetrators is not a justification for inaction.

[8]   The roman numerals in the text in the appendix (page 63 below) follow the roman numerals of the sections of the chapter.

[9]   While the Hebrew here—*nitpas*—is slightly ambiguous, a parallel source in *Bavli Avodah Zarah* 17b uses the explicit *ne'enash*, which unambiguously means "punished." Rashi interprets *nitpas* as *ne'nash* or "punished."

[10]   *Mechi* is the Aramaic word.

[11]   Mishnah Baba Bathra 2:3.

[12]   Mishnah Baba Bathra 3:6.

[13]   Bavli Avodah Zarah 17b.

[14]   In this same comment, Rashi defines the world as only referring to the Jewish people. Meiri appears not to agree with this interpretation either.

[15]   This version is translated from MS Vat. 108. The printed editions have: "As this that R. Hanina said . . ." This introductory form implies that R. Hanina's statement is some sort of proof for R. Papa's statement. This is not so, however. R. Hanina's statement deals with relations between the political and religious leadership (in simplistic terms) while R. Papa is discussing relations between Jews and the rest of the world.

[16]   Rav Papa is a fourth-century Babylonian sage.

[17]   This is, of course, the practice of midrash. This is the reading practice which is one of the hallmarks of the rabbis and the rabbinic period and textual tradition. A verse is decontextualized. It is recontextualized within another story, a verse which has an intertextual relation with it, or "Judaism" writ large. Each of its component words is then read to exploit its full semantic field, as informed by the new context. A Midrashic reading is generated by a textual anomaly, inconsistency, contradiction, real, or imagined. This type of reading is also applied to the Mishnah. On the practice of midrash, see Daniel Boyarin, *Intertextuality and the Reading of Midrash*, (Bloomington, IN: Indiana University Press, 1990).

[18]   E.g. as in Exodus 24:1

[19]   See for example, Peter Singer, "What Should a Billionaire Give—and What Should You?" in *New York Times Magazine* (December 17, 2006). See also Kwame Anthony Appiah, *Cosmopolitanism: Ethics in a World of Strangers* (New York, NY: W. W. Norton & Co., 2006).

[20]   This phrase occurs sixty-seven times in the Babylonian Talmud (according to a search of the Bar Ilan Reponsa Project version 14). It is thus a common setting for a story.

[21]   Jeffrey Rubenstein, *The Culture of the Babylonian Talmud* (Baltimore: Johns Hopkins University Press, 2003).

[22]   Sukkah 31a, Ketubot 80b, Baba Bathra 9b, Avodah Zarah 28b, Eruvin 25a—all in the Babylonian Talmud. This specific trope does not seem to appear in the Palestinian Talmud.

[23] Certain literary theorists speak of "functions" in a story. The "screaming woman" here seems to fill a pared-down version of the function of the Other, which is not to ignore that it is a woman who is cast in this role—an unsurprising move in the context of a patriarchal culture.

[24] There is a parallel to the story with some changes, though none of them significant to the point here, in the Palestinian midrash collection, Eichah Rabbah 4:3.

[25] The word is *machi*, the Aramaic form of *machah*. In the Eichah Rabbah version, it is the Hebrew *limchot*.

[26] Sometimes Zera is Rabbi Zera and sometimes Rav Zera. Either this is because he acquired official ordination at some time in his career or because there were two sages with the same name. (The medievals are split about this.) In any event, the manuscript tradition here has *R'* (i.e., just a *resh* and the apostrophe that denotes an abbreviation), so we have no way of determining. R. Zera was, according to some traditions, the student of Rav Yehudah from the previous story, so there might be some significance to his appearance here. (See, for example, b Shabbat 77b where R. Zera attests to meeting R. Yehudah and asking him a question. However, there too the manuscripts have an abbreviated *R'*, for R' Zera which could be either Rabbi or Rav. Rav Yehudah's title is spelled out.)

[27] Whether in reality as his student or as a literary device.

[28] It is not clear that they are directly victims or are merely horrified by the fact that the abominations have been done.

Appendix to Chapter 2

Mishnah Shabbat 5:4

[. . .]

A cow should not [go out on Shabbat] with the skin of a hedgehog [tied to protect its teats] or with a strap between its horns.

Rabbi Elazar ben Azaryah's cow would go out with a strap between its horns against the will of the Sages.

Bavli Shabbat 54b–55a

Did he only have one cow?

Did not Rav say (and there are those who say it was Rav Yehudah who said in the name of Rav): Rabbi Elazar ben Azaryah would tithe twelve thousand lambs each and every year!

It was taught: The cow was not his, rather it was his neighbor's. Since he did not protest [her allowing the cow out with a strap between its horns] it was named after him.

I. Rav, R. Hanina, R. Yohanan, and R. Haviva taught:

[. . .]

All who can protest against [something wrong that] one of their family [is doing] and does not protest, is held accountable for their family.

[All who can protest against something wrong that] a ci-tizen of their city [is doing and does not protest], is held account-able for all citizens of the city.

[All who can protest against something wrong that is being done] in the whole world, is accountable together with all citizens of the world.

Said R. Papa: "These of the house of the Exilarch are punished for all the world."

As this that R. Hanina said: "Why is it written: 'The LORD will enter into judgment with the elders of His people, and the princes thereof" (Isa. 3:14). If the princes sinned, what did the elders do?

Rather, say that the elders did not protest against the princes."

II. R. Yehudah was sitting in front of [i.e., was learning from] Shmuel.

A certain woman came.

She cried out before him, and he paid no attention.

He [R. Yehudah] said to him: "Does the Master not hold that *One Who stops his ears at the cry of the poor, he also shall cry himself, but shall not be answered?*" (Prov. 21:13)

He [Shmuel] said to him: "Sharp one! Your head [i.e., Shmuel] is cold. Your head's head is in the heat!

Mar Uqba is sitting as the head of the court."

For it is written: *O house of David, thus said the LORD: Execute justice in the morning, and deliver the spoiled out of the hand of the oppressor, lest My fury go forth like fire, and burn that none can quench it, because of the evil of your doings* (Jer. 21:12).

III. R. Zera said to R. Simon: "The Master should rebuke these of the house of the partriarch."

He [R. Simon] said to him: "They will not accept [the rebuke] from me."

He said to him: "Even though they will not accept it, the Master should rebuke them."

For R. Aha son of R. Hanina said: Never did a good decree leave the mouth of the Holy One of Blessing which then [the Holy One of Blessing] turned to evil except concerning this matter.

For it is written: *And God said to him, pass through the city, through Jerusalem, and make a mark on the foreheads of the men who are sighing and groaning for all the abominations that have been done in it [Jerusalem]* (Ezek. 9:4).

Said the Holy One of Blessing to Gavriel:

"Go and write on the foreheads of the righteous an ink mark so that the angels of destruction will not have power over them.

And on the foreheads of the wicked a mark of blood so that the angels of destruction shall have power over them."

Truth said to the Holy One of Blessing: "Master of the World, how are these different than these?"

God said to her: "These are completely righteous and these are completely wicked."

She said before God: "Master of the World, they were able to protest and they did not protest."

God said to her: "It is revealed and known to me that if they had protested, they would not have accepted the protest."

She said to God: "Master of the World, though it is revealed to You, is it revealed to them?"

This is what is written: *An old man, a young man, a maiden, children, women, wipe them out completely. But all who have the mark do not touch; and start with my Temple* (Ezek. 9:6).

And it also is written: *And they started with the elders in front of the House* (Ezek. 9:6).

R. Yosef taught: "Do not read 'my temple' (*mikdashi*), but rather, 'my sanctified ones' (*mekudashay*). These are people who fulfilled the Torah from Aleph to Tav."

And immediately: *And here, six people approach from the Upper Gate which faces north, and each person has their tool of destruction in their hand, and amongst them is one dressed in linens and the scribe's case is by his side. And they approached and stood beside the bronze altar* **(Ezek. 9:2).**

Chapter 3

Geographical Boundaries
and the Boundaries of Responsibility

December 24, 2002, was my forty-fourth birthday. The previous night, I had gone to the Joint, a local club in our neighborhood in Los Angeles, to celebrate together with my partner Andrea. Monday nights they had a band fronted by Waddy Wachtel, Warren Zevon's amazing guitarist. We were joined by another couple, who had initiated us into this local Monday-night happening. Being that it was the night before Christmas Eve, a number of musicians dropped by to jam with the band. It was a great night. The club was long and narrow, the music was loud and very good, there were a lot of people, and there was a lot of beer. The crowd was mature; we were definitely on the younger end of the age spectrum on this night. The show started at nine-thirty, and we were probably there till midnight.

When we left the club, it was a clear night, brisk, in the lower forties. We were in the few weeks of winter weather in Los Angeles. We parted company with our friends and walked home. The Joint is on Pico Boulevard near Robertson. The neighborhood is usually referred to as "Pico-Robertson" because of this intersection at its heart, though the real estate agents called it Beverly Hills adjacent. Pico Boulevard is a wide street with stores on both sides. During the day, contrary to widespread impressions of Los Angeles, the streets are full of people going to and from shops, supermarkets, restaurants, pizza shops, and cafés. At night, the street is mainly empty.

We crossed Pico and walked to our house along a side street. Walking south, the neighborhood is obviously residential. At first, there were many multi-unit dwellings with car parks called dingbats. Then the private houses started to predominate. Our block is all one-family and two-family houses—the latter called duplexes in Los Angeles. We live in the lower unit of a Spanish-style corner duplex. We had been there two years, feeling very lucky to have been able to buy into a very tight housing market which was getting tighter by the day.

We entered the house, walking past the lawn, the trikes and toys and plastic furniture on our patio, paid the babysitter, checked on our kids, and went to sleep. The next day, my birthday, was a lazy day. The university was closed; the semester was over. I was just back from an academic conference and thought I would get some grading done. The only thing on my calendar was a three o'clock meeting with a friend at Delice, a café on Pico.

Nine miles away, in downtown Los Angeles, life was very different for Stanley Barger. Stanley Barger suffered a brain injury in a car accident in 1998 and subsequently lost his Social Security Disability Insurance. His total monthly income consisted of food stamps and $221 in welfare payments.[1] On the night of the twenty-third of December, Barger, who could rarely afford a place even in an SRO (single-room occupancy) hotel, bedded down on the sidewalk on the corner of East Sixth Street and Towne Avenue. At 5:00 a.m., December 24, Los Angeles Police Department officers roused Barger from sleep and arrested him. The charge was violating section 41.18(d) of the Municipal Code.

Section 41.18(d) of the municipal code says the following:

> No person shall sit, lie or sleep in or upon any street, sidewalk or other public way.

Since there are not enough shelter beds to house the homeless, Section 41.18(d), which is enforced round the clock, criminalizes homelessness.[2] As I woke up on the morning of the twenty-fourth to the sounds of a raucously peaceful household, Stanley Barger was jailed—perhaps the first time that the county had provided him with shelter.

The coincidence in time of these two events provokes me to ask about my connection with Stanley Barger. I live in a city of millions. This is a city (actually a county since the city of Beverly Hills, for example, protects its wealth under the mantel of municipal independence) with the most amazing disparities of wealth. In Inglewood several families often live in a house intended for one family, while in Beverly Hills a single family might live in a house with a dining room which could comfortably house several families. In Malibu, people often earn in a day what a person in Koreatown might make at minimum wage in a year.

What is my fundamental political responsibility to Stanley Barger? I intend here not only my responsibility to give alms, but my responsibility to question why people live on the street among such great wealth. What is my responsibility to advocate for structural change so that we move toward a city in which people do not live on the street?

Peter Brown has argued that there was a significant shift in Late Antiquity regarding the way people thought about cities and philanthropy. In Roman cities, "[i]t was always the city that was, in the first instance, the recipient of gifts, or, if not the city, the civic community . . . of the city. It was never the poor. What one can call a 'civic' model of society prevailed. . . . A rich man was praised for being a *philopatris*, a 'lover of his home-city,' never for being a *philoptochos*, a 'lover of the poor.'"[3] At the same time, "The *plebs* [the general body of citizens] of Rome included many who were chronically undernourished and vulnerable to disease. They needed 'civic' bread so as to relieve their hunger. But they did not receive this bread because they were 'poor.' They received it because they could produce a *tessera*, a token that proved (in the manner of a modern passport) that they were 'citizens.'"[4]

Brown claims that the radical change to an ideology of care for the poor as a separate group—not merely as citizens who happened to be impoverished—was a change in what he calls the "aesthetics of society." This is "a sharp sense of what constituted a good society and what constituted an ugly society, namely, one that neglected the poor or treated them inappropriately."[5] This aesthetic coincided with the rise of Christianity in the Roman Empire. However, "[t]he self-image of a classical, city-bound society had to change before the 'poor' became visible as a separate group within it."[6]

The focus of care then shifted toward the poor as a group of people. Care for the poor became an act of charity as opposed to civic responsibility. There was a cost and a benefit to this. The Roman model benefited poor people along with other citizens. The line of demarcation was citizenship. Those impoverished, homeless noncitizens who lived at the margins of society were never a focus of care. The Christian model, which Brown also sees as the Jewish and Muslim model, obligated care for all poor as good works, as charity. However, there was no political thinking about the poor. Poverty was a state which should be ameliorated, but it was not a political issue nor could (should?) it be eradicated.[7]

In this chapter, I will argue that out of Rabbinic Judaism, a model of responsibility emerges which, while recognizing the poor and homeless in society—citizen and noncitizen—as groups in need of care and deserving of support and shelter, sees the answer also in political terms. The responsibility is placed on the city as a community defined by obligation toward those who reside in its boundaries. The boundaries of obligation are not the geographical boundaries of intimacy or municipality. The central argument in this chapter is that the boundaries of responsibility redraw and exceed the boundaries of intimacy, community, and municipality.

The texts that I will introduce in this chapter are grounded in a biblical ritual which attempts to adjudicate responsibility for the ownerless places in between cities, and responsibility toward people who may pass through cities anonymously. The rabbis used this biblical ritual as a grounding for the principal that the boundaries of responsibility extend beyond the geographic boundaries of intimacy—village, community, neighborhood. Living in a contemporary megalopolis, the boundaries of my extended community and neighborhood rarely have even diplomatic relations with the neighborhood in which Stanley Barger found shelter.

The Corpse: No One and Nowhere

The biblical ritual is found in Deuteronomy, chapter 21.

1   If, in the land that the LORD your God is assigning you
    to possess, someone slain is found lying in the open, the
    identity of the slayer not being known,

2   your elders and magistrates shall go out and measure the
    distances from the corpse to the nearby towns.

3   The elders of the town nearest to the corpse shall then take
    a heifer which has never been worked, which has never
    pulled in a yoke;

4   and the elders of that town shall bring the heifer down to
    an everflowing wadi, which is not tilled or sown. There,
    in the wadi, they shall break the heifer's neck.

5   The priests, sons of Levi, shall come forward; for the
    LORD your God has chosen them to minister to Him
    and to pronounce blessing in the name of the LORD, and
    every lawsuit and case of assault is subject to their ruling.

6   Then all the elders of the town nearest to the corpse shall
    wash their hands over the heifer whose neck was broken
    in the wadi.

7   And they shall make this declaration: "Our hands did not
    shed this blood, nor did our eyes see it done.

8   Absolve, O LORD, Your people Israel whom You
    redeemed, and do not let guilt for the blood of the
    innocent remain among Your people Israel." And they
    will be absolved of bloodguilt.

9   Thus you will remove from your midst guilt for the blood
    of the innocent, for you will be doing what is right in the
    sight of the LORD.

The opening verse of the section frames the incident as
involving both a body whose identity is not known and also a place
which is not accounted for by any specific municipal authority. The
word translated as "open space" is the Hebrew *sadeh* which is often
opposed to inhabited spaces and has the connotation of ownerless
or wild.[8]

There are three stages to the ritual once the body is found.[9]
First, a measurement is conducted to determine which town is
closest and therefore will bear at the least symbolic responsibility.
Then the elders of that town will bring the offering to the riverbed.[10]
They finally perform the ritual itself. The elders break the neck of the
animal, they wash their hands over the animal, and they recite the
formula: "Our hands did not shed this blood, nor did our eyes see it
done. Absolve, O LORD, Your people Israel whom You redeemed,

and do not let guilt for the blood of the innocent remain among Your people Israel." The Torah seems intent on taking a crime which happened to no one—the victim is just referred to as "the corpse" or "someone slain"—in the middle of nowhere and making the statement that there is always someone who is responsible, someone who must expiate the blood.[11]

The Mishnah

A whole chapter of Mishnah is devoted to this ritual—the last chapter of Tractate Sotah.[12] The chapter of Mishnah interrogates every point of possible ambiguity in the biblical ritual. What if the man is not found on the ground but in a tree? Where on the body do you measure from? The head? The navel? What happens if one witness claims to have seen the murderer, while the second witness claims to have not seen the murderer.[13] What happens to the animal if after it was brought to the stream, yet before it was killed, the killer was found? The questions continue on and on.

The sages of the Mishnah are also intrigued by the formula which the elders of the town are to say at the climactic moment of the ritual:

Mishnah Sotah 9:6

The elders of that town wash their hands in the water at the place of the killing of the heifer, and they say: "Our hands did not spill this blood, and are our eyes did not see."

And did we believe that the elders[14] of the court are spillers of blood?

Rather [they say]: "For he did not come to us and we dismissed him. And we did not see him and let him be."[15]

The Mishnah reads the formula hyperliterally in order to ask the disturbing question: Why is it that the elders of the town are instructed to disavow their guilt? Was there actually a presumption that they were in fact guilty?

Essentially, the Mishnaic author is reading the verse "midrashically." This means that he is reading the verse strongly to press on the literal problematics in the verse. In this instance, it seems that the irritant is the fact that the second half of the verse, "and our eyes did not see," does not have an object for the verb "see." Most modern translations supply the missing object from the first half of the statement. That is, as the JPS translation has it, "nor did our eyes see it done." The King James translation and others[16] just add the word "it."[17]

The Mishnah seems to have read this naked verb strongly as intransitive—a verb without an object. That is, the elders of the town must declare that they were not guilty of not seeing, of willful or negligent blindness—and that that blindness led to the shedding of the blood. A paraphrase of the declaration as the Mishnah is now reading it would be, "We were not willfully or negligently blind and thereby caused this bloodshed." This reading of the verse in Deuteronomy is played out in the rhetorical question: "Did we ever think that the elders of the court are spillers of blood?" Which allows the answer: "Rather they must say: 'For he did not come to us and we dismissed him. And we did not see him and let him be.'"

This reading of the ritual declaration from Deuteronomy is strengthened in the discussion of this Mishnah in the Babylonian Talmud.

The Talmudic Discussion

The Talmudic discussion of this Mishnah begins by citing a *baraita*. A baraita is, literally, an "outside text."[18] It is a text whose authority and provenance are similar to the Mishnah, though they were "left out" of the canonical collection of Mishnah attributed to Rabbi Judah the Patriarch. This particular baraita comments on Deuteronomy 21:6–7. Our interest lies in the second half of the baraita, the comment on Deuteronomy 21:7:

> "And they shall make this declaration: 'Our hands did not shed this blood, nor did our eyes see it done.'
> And did we believe that the court [is composed of] murderers? Rather [they say] "He did not come to us and we dismissed him with no food," and "We did not see him and yet leave him with no escort."

The comments of this text take the Mishnah's midrashic reading of Deuteronomy 21:7 one step further. The author of this baraita explains what is meant by "dismissed him" and "let him be." The former refers to not providing the Stranger with food and letting him sally forth on his own, hungry. In the eleventh century, Rashi (Rabbenu Shlomo Yitzhaki) poignantly commented, "This is what is meant by 'our hands did not spill . . .' he was not killed as a result of our action that we dismissed him without food, and he was forced to steal from people and was killed as a result of that." Rashi adds another narrative layer in trying to imagine what the exact events leading to death were. The counterfactual story, the story that the elders are disavowing, is that a stranger comes to town, does not find any food, and leaves empty-handed, alone, and hungry. Desperate for food, he attempts to rob another wayfarer and is killed in the attempt. The detail in this story, which we swear did not happen, pushes us to begin to suspect that it might, in fact, have happened. This is what the literary theorist Jacques Derrida calls "writing under erasure"[19]—introducing something into the conversation and immediately negating it, in the manner of saying "Johnny is not sick" rather than "Johnny is well." Saying "Johnny is not sick" places the idea of sickness in the conversation (as if one said "Johnny is sick").

This is true here. The elders, the representatives of the city, relate this narrative, "This stranger came to us and we dismissed him without food and he was forced to rob another person and was killed in the process," by denying it: The counterfactual details, the facts of the case that are disavowed, continue, "We let him be without providing an escort for him." It is not true, the elders protest, that we were blind to his plight. The growing facts of the disavowed narrative lead us to the conclusion that there is actual responsibility here. Somebody should have seen. What kind of place is this which a stranger can wander through in total anonymity and not be offered food and provided with escort? Therefore, the court, the institution that defines a settlement as a city,[20] has to atone for this death.

The feeling of responsibility is immediately translated into legislation as the Talmudic discussion continues, citing another baraita.

> Rabbi Meir would say: We coerce accompaniment, for the
> reward for accompaniment has no measure.

This is the final step in articulating the responsibility placed upon the
city. In the Deuteronomic ritual, we first find the elders responsible
because of geographic location to the blood impurity which must
be purged. ("Your brother's blood cries out to me from the soil."
Gen. 4:10) The Mishnah assigns a more specific responsibility which
the baraita thickens. A stranger passing through town is owed, it
seems, food and protection. Finally, Rabbi Meir codifies this responsibility.

The "coercion" of Rabbi Meir's statement implies that there
are judicial institutions in the background able to enforce the law.
In the twelfth century, Maimonides articulated this responsibility
in his great code of Jewish Law, the *Mishneh Torah*: "We coerce
accompaniment as we coerce alms-giving;[21] the court would appoint
agents to accompany a person who was traveling from one place to
another."[22]

Lest we have too domesticated a view of what coercion is, the
early modern commentator *Maharsh"a*, Rabbi Shlomo Eidels (1555–
1631) points to Tractate Hullin 110b.

> They brought a man who was not honoring his father and
> mother.
> They tied him up.
> He said to them: Leave him be. For it is taught [in a baraita]
> The court is not enjoined [to enforce] any positive
> commandment whose reward is indicated explicitly [in
> Torah].

This short story is told in a series of stories whose aim is to show
how bright a certain Rami bar Tamri from Pumbeditha is. Rami
(the "He" who says "Leave him be.") frees the man because of
the principle that the court need not force one to observe a commandment whose reward is explicitly stated in the Torah. The
commandment to honor one's parents in the Decalogue, Exodus
20:12, is followed by the announcement of the reward for observance
of the command. "Honor your father and your mother in order that
your days may be prolonged on the soil which God, your God gives

to you."[23] The fact that the reward is stated, removes the obligation (or right) of the court to coerce observance of the law.

Rashi explains what the coercion might look like: "a positive commandment which presents itself to a person, and he does not want to fulfill it; for example, they say to him 'make a Succah' and he does not make it . . . they beat him until his soul departs." This, according to Eidels, is what "coercion" is. It is not peer pressure or religious guilt. It is not even "moderate physical force" to use a current euphemism. It is violent persuasion. Not that the full force of the violent persuasion needs be deployed in every given situation. However, the possibility of the full force of institutional judicial coercion hovers in the background of any discussion.

This move, that we just outlined above, from purging blood guilt to accepting municipal responsibility for strangers and which is traced from Torah to the statement of Rabbi Meir, is accompanied by another move. The story and ritual in Deuteronomy focuses on the *sadeh*, the ownerless space between towns. The statement of the elders as now understood focuses on what happens in cities. Only cities which have a court are considered under this legislation,[24] and it is the city (or, for Maimonides explicitly, the court) which bears the responsibility. The baraita and Rabbi Meir's statement move us directly into the urban arena. The Talmud is no longer concerned with what happened on the road. The concern is with what happened in the city, and what will happen in the city in the future.

Let us attend to Rabbi Meir's statement in some greater detail.

"We Coerce Accompaniment"

There are two parts to Rabbi Meir's statement. The first part is as just stated, "We coerce[25] accompaniment." There seems to be an internal contradiction in this phrase itself. Accompaniment is often an intimate act. One accompanies a friend home after dinner. One accompanies a lover to a play. Less anachronistically, one accompanies a sage to the study hall and back as a sign of respect and love. Why then does Rabbi Meir say that we *coerce* accompaniment? This then is obviously not (only) the intimate accompaniment of friends and lovers, or even of students and teachers, but the accompaniment of strangers, the accompaniment of those for whom the city takes responsibility since there is not necessarily a single person who otherwise would take responsibility.

This contradiction is apparent in Maimonides's discussion of accompaniment in his code, *Mishneh Torah*. In the paragraph preceding the one we discussed above,[26] Maimonides lauds accompaniment along with hospitality:

> The reward for accompaniment is greater than all. This is the law which Abraham legislated, and the path of grace which he practiced. He would feed the wayfarers, give them to drink and accompany them [as they left]. Taking in guests is greater than receiving the face of the Holy Presence . . ., and accompanying them is greater than taking them in.[27]

It is the Abrahamic vision which is projected as the ideal of hospitality. The tent is open to all four sides, and everyone who passes by stops in and is given sustenance. This is a vision of deep care and altruism. Yet this is the law which Abraham carved in stone.[28] In the move from the individual actions of an iconically just patriarch to the multifaceted tensions and contradictions of a city, the care for the Stranger could no longer rely on the omniscience of individuals. There is too much risk of inaction, of indifference. The city as a body needs to be able to delegate obligations to individuals in order to maintain the justice of the whole.[29]

We now read the second half of the statement. "For the reward for accompaniment has no measure." If the reward for accompanying a stranger has no measure, why would there be a need to coerce someone to do it? The logic of the text we just cited from Hullin 110b[30] is that if a commandment has an obvious reward, there is no need for coercion.[31] While the reward for accompaniment might not appear explicitly in the Torah, it is explicit in Rabbi Meir's statement.

Rabbi Meir's statement highlights the fact that accompaniment is part of two discourses. On the one hand, it is a matter of personal piety, for which the reward has no measure; it is immeasurably large.[32] This is the individual attempting to follow in the footsteps of Abraham. On the other hand, there is the matter of justice in the polis. The city as a community which is based on relations of justice has an obligation to the Stranger. This obligation devolves upon any or every specific individual as a limb of the communal body.

Levayah—accompanying or escorting—occurs in one other context which might shed some light on the structure of the gesture itself. The only other usage of the term levayah is in the discussion in the Babylonian Talmud Berachot 18a of the obligation to accompany a dead person on the way to burial.

> Said Rahbah said R. Yehudah: Anyone who sees a dead person and does not accompany it, transgresses upon: "He who mocks the poor, affronts his Maker" (Prov. 17:5).
> And if he does escort, what is his reward? Said R. Asi: About him Scripture says: "He who is generous to the poor makes a loan to the Lord" (Prov. 19:17). "He who shows pity for the needy honors Him" (Prov. 14:31).

Again here the stakes are ultimate, beyond measure. If one does not accompany a dead person, it is God that one is insulting. On the other hand, if one does accompany the dead, one has God in one's debt.[33]

The levayah of the dead also reinforces the basic structure of accompaniment. It is a reaching out toward another, a gesture which has no hope of being repaid. It is not a gift in the anthropological sense—a gesture which creates an obligation.[34] It is only an answer to a commanding of the Other, the Stranger in the Levinasian sense.[35]

The obligation to accompany another is an obligation to cross boundaries. In accompanying the dead, the boundaries that are crossed are those between life and death. The gesture is not one that is dependent on a sense of mutuality since there is no possibility that the dead will repay the kindness. Accompaniment is a stretching across fixed boundaries, whether of a city or of life.

This movement of stretching across boundaries (especially the impermeable boundary between life and death) moves the conversation into the realm of the fantastic. The distinguishing feature of the fantastic as a literary genre is an uncertainty or a hesitation experienced by the reader. "The fantastic is that hesitation experienced by a person who knows only the laws of nature confronting an apparently supernatural event."[36] The fantastic functions only in the context of the normal workings of the universe. "The fantastic is always a break in the acknowledged order, an irruption of the inadmissible within the changeless everyday legality."[37] Within a work of fiction, the intervention of the supernatural in life constitutes a break "in the system of pre-established rules."[38]

I want to suggest that accompaniment presages just this "irruption of the inadmissible within the changeless everyday legality." One might even be tempted to read the phrase, "it has no measure" as meaning that the effects of accompanying the Stranger are unknown, are beyond the simple causality of the day to day. The assumption of the obligation of accompaniment by the city and its performance by an individual serves to redraw the boundaries of a city. The boundaries of the city are no longer the geographical boundaries or the cartographical boundaries. They are the boundaries of responsibility. These boundaries lie well beyond the boundaries of intimate geography which define most of our communities. The gesture of accompaniment points toward, or is in fact, a reaching through or stretching of the boundaries of intimacy which are usually defined by hospitality.

We find this explicitly in the discussion of accompanying the dead, *levayat hamet*, in Tractate Berachot. The discussion in Berachot 18a continues from the initial charge to accompany the dead with stories of the "courtyard of death" in which the dead and living meet, and the dead can teach the living. Escorting the dead leads to crossing the boundaries which separate the living from the dead.[39]

We find the same rhetorical move here in our text in Sotah. Rabbi Meir's statement is followed by a prooftext:

> For it says: "Their watchmen saw a man leaving the town. They said to him: 'Just show us how to get into the town, and we will treat you kindly'" (Judg. 1:24).
> And it is written: "He showed them how to get into the town" (Judg. 1:25).

What was the kindness that they did with him? They put the whole town to the sword, but they sent away the man and his family.

"The man went to the Hittite country. He founded a city and named it Luz, and that had been its name to this day" (Judg. 1:26).

The prooftext draws upon a short incident in the first chapter of the book of Judges.

23   While the House of Joseph were scouting at Bethel (the name of the town was formerly Luz),

24   their patrols saw a man leaving the town. They said to him, "Just show us how to get into the town, and we will treat you kindly."

25   He showed them how to get into the town; they put the town to the sword, but they let the man and all his relatives go free.

26   The man went to the Hittite country. He founded a city and named it Luz, and that has been its name to this day.

Verse 24, in which the patrols implore the man to show them the entrance to the city and in exchange "we will treat you kindly," is cited as the verse on which R. Meir bases his law. The reasoning behind this is that the scouts promised the man kindness in exchange for his betraying his own city. After the betrayal, the kindness is granted — while everyone else is slaughtered, the man and his family are saved. The end of verse 26 — "and that has been its name *to this day*" — is being read here to explicate "without measure." If the city exists to this very day, it must truly be a fantastic place beyond rational bounds. Indeed, the Talmud immediately cites a baraita to this very effect:

This is Luz where they make the blue dye for the fringes;[40]
this is Luz to where Sennacharib came but did not mix her up;[41]
Nebuchadnezer came but did not destroy her.
Even the angel of death has no permission to pass there.
Rather, the elders of the city, when they have had enough of life,[42] they exit the wall [of the city] and they die.

This story reinforces the ambiguity of the reward for accompaniment. It strengthens the question: "Is the reward boundless or unspecified or unpredictable?" Here, in the rabbinic reading of the story from Judges, the reward is double-edged. The man himself is saved with his family. Moreover, he gets to live in a place that is beyond time, beyond death. It is a place that borders upon the world of death, but it itself is immune. Death happens when those in its borders choose to pass over into the realm of death. On the other hand, the price paid was the extinction of the rest of the population of the city which he had betrayed.

The most striking thing about this prooftext is that it doesn't seem to *prove* anything. The man did not *accompany* the watchmen; he merely showed them the entrance to the city. He was also showing them how to get *into* the city, rather than accompanying them out of the city. The Talmud itself sensed these difficulties.

> If this Canaanite—who did not talk with his mouth, nor did he walk with his legs—brought about salvation for himself and his descendants until the end of the generations;
> How much the more so for one who [actually] accompanies one by foot?!

This is the anonymous voice of the Talmud—the *stam*—commenting on the earlier statement and prooftext of Rabbi Meir.[43] The stam's solution is to claim that the import of the prooftext is that accompaniment is so powerful a commandment that even one who barely fulfills the command is rewarded with such munificence. This then is proof that the reward is "beyond measure" for those who actually accompany.

I would suggest that we read this prooftext differently. The point of the prooftext is not the reward of the watchman but the connection with that which is beyond death. Again, as in escorting the dead, accompaniment is linked to the ultimate boundary crossing, or, more importantly, to reaching beyond the seemingly most fixed boundaries. The watchmen get into the city, which is otherwise impenetrable; the man goes to another city, which exists in a space which is beyond death, but the residents of the town can negotiate this boundary between life and death at will—even though the angel of death cannot. Thus, it is the fantastic which is used to describe the possibilities that are envisioned by the legal obligation.[44] The direct analogue is that the possibility of a city in which accompaniment of the Stranger is an obligation on all residents is a city whose map of responsibility does not abide by the boundaries of its municipal map. It is a city in which there is no *sadeh*—no ownerless place toward which there is no responsibility.

Politics

Emmanuel Levinas argued for the importance of grounding philosophical speculation in the initial gesture of recognizing the Other—any other person—as being beyond my grasp. That is, he claimed that the Western philosophical tradition "knew" the world by describing it with categories which originate in the knower. In essence, then, the task of knowing was to successfully assimilate the Other into the Same, that is the knower or me.

This might seem to be a good way to go philosophically for a while. If I want to know what exists in the world, I create large categories of things (flowers, plants, planets, TV shows) and then slowly distinguish between the huge number of objects in each category by the subtler differences between them. Thus I am not left with an undifferentiated laundry list of stuff that happens to be in the world. I have a way of grasping what those objects are. What I am doing at base is bringing those objects into my categories so they become familiar. I am bridging or breaking the intellectual gap between them and me. Hence I am assimilating that which is other, different, not me, into that which is the same—that is, me and my intellectual concepts.

Knowing an object in this way does, however, deny the object any uniqueness. A unique object cannot ever really be known—just as the way we must guess at the meaning of Hebrew words which only occur once in the Torah. If there is no category in which to place the object, then there is no way to differentiate it from some other category.

This is, perhaps, all fine and well for inanimate objects. However, Levinas argues, the basic characteristic of a person is that he or she is unique. Or, to use Levinas's terminology, a person is an "infinity." This is opposed to those other objects which are a "totality," meaning that we can grasp them *in toto*. The problem then is that if we want to know the world, perhaps the most important or at least the closest, part of that world that we want to know cannot be described by category and difference. The basic characteristic of another person, the Other, is that they are ungraspable, an "infinity." They cannot be completely grasped. Then, if I do breach the chasm that exists between me (the "same") and you (the "Other"), I have misunderstood you. If I place the Other in a category and I define the Other by difference, I have by definition misdefined the Other.

The only possible engagement with the Other is response. The relationship is not equal; it is hierarchical with the Other always in the transcendent position. It is also not mutual. I do not respond to you because I expect that you will then respond to me.

For Levinas, this philosophical move, which is at heart *also* an ethical move, is the bulwark against totalitarianism which is the highest form of assimilating the Other into the Same, or denuding the Other of individuality and treating all others as cogs in a wheel, which is the same thing.

As I've described it, this is an ethics of intimacy. This is a powerful way of describing and conceptualizing relationships between two individuals so that I do not profess to ever be able to know you to the extent that I might be tempted to use you.[45] The model, however, stumbles on the political.[46] This is sometimes referred to as the problem of the third. If there are three people in a relationship (and on *ad infinitum*), who is responding to whom? As a political model, it seems unworkable.[47]

Accompaniment as a conceptual frame offers a solution. Apart from my obligation to respond to the Other, the city as a community of residents has an obligation to the Stranger. The city mediates this obligation in the form of delegating responsibility to residents. "We coerce accompaniment." The reward for accompaniment is that my neighborhood or community does not have impermeable boundaries, rather I am bound by the logic of the city's obligation to Stanley Barger to cross those boundaries.

Walking the Talk

The logic of levayah/accompaniment says that the justness of a city is a function of the web of relationships between "strangers," between people who are anonymous to each other. If people can fall into a place which is beyond anybody's responsibility, this is a reflection on the justness of the city itself. This is when the city needs to atone.

The performance of accompaniment as a practice exists for both the individual and the city. The actual accompaniment of guests out of one's house as the invoking of the Abrahamic ideal is a token of remembrance that the boundaries of responsibility extend beyond the boundaries of intimacy. In our daily lives, the practice of reaching out beyond ourselves is also a performance of accompaniment. Finally, in the life of a city, when budgets are being decided upon, when scarce resources are being allocated, the response to the Stranger has to be the center of the discussion. Eradicating the existence of the "ownerless places" has to be the first and not the last priority. The very fact of widespread homelessness, of people suffering and dying because they cannot afford health care, of people going hungry, shatters the illusion that we live in a just society.[48]

Chapter 3: The Boundaries of Responsibility

Notes

[1]   *Edward Jones et al. Plaintiffs-Appellants vs. City of Los Angeles et al.*; Defendants-Appellees. No. 04-55324 United States Court of Appeals for the Ninth Circuit 444 F.3d 1118; 2006 U.S. App. LEXIS 9308, pp. 13–14.

[2]   This was the opinion of the majority of the Ninth Circuit court (ibid.).

[3]   Peter Brown, *Poverty and Leadership in the Later Roman Empire* (University Press of New England, 2002), 5.

[4]   See note 3.

[5]   Peter Brown, "Remembering the Poor and the Aesthetic of Society," *Journal of Interdisciplinary History,* xxxv:3 (Winter, 2005): 514–515.

[6]   See note 5.

[7]   This shift might explain the disdain that one can read in the question of Tinnius Rufus, Akiva's interlocutor in the Babylonian Talmud Baba Bathra 10a: "If your God loves the poor, why does he not support them?"

[8]   The Rabbinic term *hefqer*/ownerless might apply. Cf. Gen. 27:3, 34:28, 37:15, Deut. 22:25, 27.

[9]   The history of this text is somewhat complicated. I will not go into it since I am interested here only in the rabbinic reception and transvaluation of the text. On the historical question, see Ziony Zevit, "The *'egla* Ritual of Deuteronomy 21:1–9," *Journal of Biblical Literature* 95 (1976): 377–390. Interestingly, some of the conflicting ideologies reflected in the textual stratification are also reflected in debates among the medieval commentaries. See Nachamanides, commentary to Deuteronomy 21:5; and Maimonides, *Guide of the Perplexed,* III:40.

[10]   The phrase translated in the JPS Tanakh as everflowing wadi is the Hebrew *nachal eitan* which can be and has been translated as "rough valley" (King James), "wadi with running water" (New Revised Standard Version), "valley with running water" (Revised Standard Version). The symbolism of the ritual is of course different if the river has water in it or not.

[11]   There is of course much more to this text. See the literature cited by Zevit. See also the discussion in the *Encylopedia Mikrait, s.v. 'eglah 'arufah,* vol. 77–78. There is a very strong resonance with the slaying of Abel by Cain which also happened in the *sadeh.* Cf. Gen. 4:8.

[12]   *Sotah* is the ritual of the suspected adulteress which is found in Numbers 5:11–31. The first six chapters of Mishnah Sotah deal with the Sotah ritual itself. Chapter 7 is a bridge by way of discussing all the rituals which must be declaimed in Hebrew. Sotah is one of these and the broken-necked heifer or the *eglah* ritual is another. It is discussed in chapter 9 of Mishnah Sotah.

[13]   Rabbinic law demands two witnesses.

[14]   MS Florence does not have "the elders" just "that the court."

¹⁵   The Mishnah text is cited according to the MSS (Kaufman, Parma, Low). The printed editions have apparently assimilated the *baraita* cited in the Bavli into the Mishnah itself. See the *baraita* on page 72 below.

¹⁶   The old JPS translation, the Revised Standard Version, and the New Revised Standard Version.

¹⁷   The ancient Greek translation known as the Septuagint and Everett Fox's contemporary translation both leave the verb bare without object.

¹⁸   Aramaic *bar*=outside.

¹⁹   Jacques Derrida, *Of Grammatology*, trans. Gayatri Chakravorty Spivak (Johns Hopkins University Press, 1998).

²⁰   cf. Mishnah Sotah 9:2: "If he was found next to . . . a city which had no court, they would not do the ritual. We only measure from a city which has a co-urt." It is the *existence* of the court which defines a place as a *city* which is to be held responsible.

²¹   This statement itself, "we coerce alms-giving/*tzedakah*" is of great importance. I translated *tzedakah* as alms-giving rather than charity in order to destabilize the altruistic relationship which is implied by "charity" coming from the Greek *charitas* meaning "grace." (Although according to the OED, "alms" does seem to come from the Greek *eleimosunei*, meaning compassionateness, the impact is perhaps less immediate because of the anachronism.) *Tzedakah*, linguistically and ethically is derived from justice/*tzedek*.

²²   *Laws of Mourning* 14:3 (my translation).

²³   Fox translation.

²⁴   See note 20 above.

²⁵   This coercion is the same as that we saw in the discussion of the gate house in chapter 1.

²⁶   Page 74 above.

²⁷   *Laws of Mourning* 14:2.

²⁸   The literal meaning of *haqaq*, which we translated as "legislated," is "carved." *Hoq*, derived from *haqaq*, means "law."

²⁹   Jacques Derrida points out and works through some of the contradictions between hospitality as a law and hospitality as a "right of residence" in the essay "On Cosmopolitanism" in *On Cosmopolitanism and Forgiveness* (London and New York: Routledge, 2001).

³⁰   Page 74 above.

³¹   This is the question that prompted the remarks of the *Maharsha*.

³²   This understanding of "has no measure" as immeasurably large is not certain. It could also mean the reward for accompanying is unknown. The latter

understanding is the result of reading the phrase *ayn lah shiur*/it has no measure through the filter of a discussion of visiting the sick in b Nedarim 39b.

The discussion there is centered on a *baraita* which states, "Visiting the sick has no measure." What, the anonymous voice asks, does "has no measure" mean? R. Yosef is cited as suggesting that it means that there is no measure to the reward obtained for visiting the sick. Abbaye challenges R. Yosef with the question: "Do all commandments have a measure to their reward?"

Abbaye's challenge to R. Yosef here is exactly on our point. Is there ever a commandment whose reward is quantified? The discussion there ultimately ends with the statement that the *obligation* of visiting the sick is unlimited. Other texts (e.g., b Menachot 41b) seem to indicate that it is possible that the phrase "has no measure" can also be understood in the reverse direction—there is no bottom limit. However, the understanding of "has no measure" as immeasurably large is well documented (e.g., Mishnah Peah 1:1) and more than plausible here.

[33] Cf. my discussion of this *sugya* in "Representation of Death in the Bavli," *AJS Review* vol. 24, no. 1 (1999): 45–71.

[34] The anthropological literature on gifts is enormous. Much of it was generated by Marcel Mauss, *The Gift: Forms and Functions of Exchange in Archaic Societies*, translated by Ian Cunnison; with an introduction by E. E. Evans-Pritchard, (New York: Norton, 1967).

[35] Emmanuel Levinas, *Totality and Infinity: An Essay on Exteriority*, trans. Alphonso Lingis (Pittsburgh: Duquesne University Press, 1969), 39.

[36] Tzvetan Todorov, *The Fantastic: A Structural Approach to a Literary Genre* (Cornell University Press, 1980), 25. Although forty years old (the first French edition, that is), this work is still the touchstone in the field. See Lucie Armitt, *Theorizing the Fantastic* (Arnold, 1996), 30–36.

[37] Ibid., 26 quoting Roger Callois.

[38] Ibid., 166; See also Michel Foucault, "A Preface to Transgression," in *Language, Memory Counter-Practice*, ed. and trans. Donald F. Bouchard, (Basil Blackwell, 1977).

[39] Note 33 above.

[40] Cf. Num. 15.

[41] Cf. Tosefta Kiddushin 5:6.

[42] Lit., when their thought is repugnant to them.

[43] It is not clear whether the prooftext is intended to be part of Rabbi Meir's statement or not. In any event, it is all part of the *baraita*, which is, of course, an earlier layer of textuality than the editor.

[44] Cf. "Law is the bridge between the is and the ought, when we recognize that both the is and the ought are narratives. Law is also that which 'licenses' those actions which are performed in order to transform the is into the ought, or the

present into the eschatological future." Robert Cover, "Nomos and Narrative," in *Narrative, Violence, and the Law: The Essays of Robert Cover*, edited by Martha Minow, Michael Ryan, and Austin Sarat,(Ann Arbor: The University of Michigan Press, 1992): 10; and "I have argued not only that the nature of law is a bridge to the future, but also that each community builds its bridges with the materials of sacred narrative that take as their subject much more than what is commonly conceived as the "legal." Robert Cover, "The Folktales of Justice: Tales of Jurisdiction," in *Narrative, Violence, and the Law: The Essays of Robert Cover*, edited by Martha Minow, Michael Ryan, and Austin Sarat (Ann Arbor: The University of Michigan Press, 1992): 177.

[45] Note the range of meanings of "to grasp."

[46] It is interesting that Levinas describes the political as the innovation of the Greeks. See our discussion of Peter Brown above, page 68-69.

[47] See my further discussion of the problem of the third within the context of homelessness in chapter 5.

[48] The Ninth Circuit majority opinion in favor of the appellants was very narrow. "All we hold is that, so long as there is a greater number of homeless individuals in Los Angeles than the number of available beds, the city may not enforce Section 41.18(d) at all times and places throughout the city against homeless individuals for involuntarily sitting, lying, and sleeping in public. Appellants are entitled at a minimum to a narrowly tailored injunction against the city's enforcement of Section 41.18(d) at certain times and/or places." *Edward Jones et al. vs. City of Los Angeles* 1138. In a July 2009 study released by the National Law Center on Homelessness and Poverty and the National Coalition for the Homeless called "Homes Not Handcuffs: The Criminalization of Homelessness in U.S. Cities" (http://nationalhomeless.org/publications/crimreport/index.html accessed on August 14, 2009) Los Angeles ranked as number one in a list of "meanest cities" (p. 33). This refers to cities that "do not provide enough affordable housing, shelter space, and food to meet the need," yet they "use the criminal justice system to punish people living on the street for doing things that they need to do to survive."

Chapter 4

A Summary of the Argument So Far

Before proceeding to some particulars of the community of obligation, I will weave together the strands of the argument so far. A just city, a city that is defined as a community of obligation, is a polis in which the residents open themselves to the possibility of hearing the cries of the Stranger—and being compelled by those cries to respond. This goes beyond directly responding to another person who crosses your path. The obligation is first, to set up our cities such that others' needs will be urgently pressing upon the body politic—whether the vulnerability that demands our response be a result of poverty, ethnicity, lack of a home, or lack of citizenship.[1] In other words, the city needs to be organized such that the cry of the Stranger can be heard. Homelessness must be decriminalized, economic segregation must be ameliorated.[2]

Second, as a practice of both politics and piety, we ought to treat others as members of our community. This can be expressed in actions on both the quotidian or immediate and the more abstract levels. The practice of accompanying guests (levayah) out of our houses, beyond the doorways and into the street, might serve as a ritual reminder that the boundary of obligation exceeds geographic boundaries. When a panhandler asks for money, we should stop and ask for her name, engage in small talk, and treat her as a member of our community toward whom we have an obligation.[3] At the same time, the obligation of levayah/accompaniment demands that we hear the concerns of those whose paths we will never cross as we act politically. Decisions on budgets and zoning are more obviously ethical decisions, but so too are decisions about what restaurants or markets we patronize, what hotels we stay at, and how we treat the people who clean our houses and watch our children.[4] These issues are all interconnected since where you live can also determine whether or not you will have access to healthy food and health care, whether your children will suffer from diabetes or obesity, and whether you will have access to a job that pays a living wage.[5]

The web of relationships which results from the desire to respond to the (anonymous) other in the community of obligation also leads to the demand that residents protest against injustice. The rabbinic version of the saying, "Injustice anywhere is injustice everywhere," is the more activist demand that "[a]ll who can protest against [something wrong that] one of their family [is doing] and does not protest, is accountable together with their family. [All who can protest against something wrong that] a citizen of their city [is doing and does not protest], is accountable together with all citizens of the city. [All who can protest against something wrong that is being done] in the whole world, is accountable together with all citizens of the world." This demand is that, in a community of obligation, the demands of righting that which is wrong is not predicated on an ethics of intimacy but stems, rather, from the absolute responsibility of each person for justice in the world.

In the second half of the book, I will explore the way in which these larger principles play out in the context of the more concrete issues of homelessness, labor relations, and restorative justice.

Notes

[1]   I do not directly address the issue of residents of a polis who are not citizens. Undocumented residents, however, at this moment in the United States, are the most present example of the strangers we refuse to hear. For now, see Avishai Margalit, *The Decent Society,* trans. Naomi Goldblum (Harvard University Press, 1998) chapter 9, and especially "Since a decent society involves respect for humans, and humiliating any human being is wrong, no distinction should be made in this regard between members of the society and people in its orbit who are not members" (p. 150). While Margalit's notion of a "decent society" is not the same as the community of obligation, Margalit himself limns the concept of a decent as a necessary prerequisite to a just society (p. ix).

[2]   On homelessness, see my discussion in chapter 1 of the second part of the book. On mixed income or inclusionary zoning, see, for example, Urban Land Institute, *Mixed Income Housing Advisory Group: Workforce Housing Options in Los Angeles Considerations for the City of Los Angeles* (Draft) December 2008, http://www.

uli-la.org/files/Workforce-Housing-Options-for-Los-Angeles-Draft.pdf (accessed August 23, 2010).

[3] Going beyond this, my colleague Ariella Radwin suggests the practice of having water on hot days to distribute to panhandlers at street corners. Radwin attributes this practice to Tobin Belzer, another colleague (personal communication).

[4] Cf. Jim Wallis's statement at a Brookings Institution panel: "Budgets are moral documents. They reveal the priorities, the values of a family, a church, a synagogue, a city, a state, or a nation. What is important? What is not? Who is important? Who is not? This is a moral conversation, also a very practical one." "Restoring America's Promise of Opportunity, Prosperity and Growth" (2006), p. 20.

[5] See "Feeding Our Communities: A Call for Standards for Food Access and Job Quality in Los Angeles's Grocery Industry" (Los Angeles: Blue Ribbon Commission on LA's Grocery Industry and Community Health, 2008).

PART II

Chapter 5

Homelessness

"There are among them many worthless creatures, no doubt who would sooner beg than work, but the greater part of them are evidently legitimate objects of charity, and their necessities should be attended to. The Police should have strict orders given them to arrest and send to the station-houses, every person, man woman or child who may be found begging in the streets. ... Every citizen has to contribute too largely to the support of the poor, both by public and private taxes, to be subjected to the incessant annoyances of these mendicants who swarm in all our streets, and haunt our dwelling-houses and places of business."

New York Times (November 26, 1857), p. 4.

"Weary of shelters, the couple pitched a pup tent in Roger Williams Park, close to a plaque bearing words Williams [the founder of Rhode Island] had used to describe this place he founded: "A Shelter for Persons in Distress." But someone complained, so Mr. Freitas set off again in search of shelter. The March winds blew."

"Living in Tents, and by the Rules, Under a Bridge," Dan Barry, *New York Times* (July 31, 2009).

At the most intense moment of the Jewish liturgical year—Yom Kippur/the fast of the Day of Atonement—the tradition dictates that the portion that we read from the prophets, the *haftarah*, is one that challenges the very practice embodied in that holy fast day. The reader chants the words of Isaiah, as Isaiah channels the fury of God: "Is this the kind of fast I have chosen, only a day for a man to humble himself? . . . Is it not to share your food with the hungry and to provide the poor wanderer with shelter . . . !"

Contrary to some popular misconceptions, Isaiah is not dismissing ritual as so much folderol. At the end of that same chapter, he says, "If you refrain from trampling the Sabbath, from pursuing your affairs on My holy day; If you call the Sabbath 'delight,' The LORD's holy day 'honored'; And if you honor it and go not your ways nor look to your affairs, nor strike bargains— Then you can seek the favor of the LORD. I will set you astride the heights of the earth, And let you enjoy the heritage of your father Jacob. . . ." Rather, feeding the hungry and providing shelter for the homeless (together with clothing the naked) are established as the prerequisites of righteousness. It is impossible, Isaiah says, for an individual to make a claim on piety without first having passed this threshold.

What, however, is the threshold? In this chapter, we will analyze the development of an obligation toward the homeless from a personal to a communal obligation.

Prerequisites for Piety

I want to focus on one phrase of Isaiah's speech which I mentioned at the beginning of this chapter: "and to provide the poor wanderer with shelter. . . ." Where is this sentiment translated into the language of obligation, commitment, or public policy? In examining the texts from the third-century Mishnah, the sixth-century Babylonian Talmud, and the twelfth- and thirteenth-century commentary tradition on the Talmud, we will see that there is an interesting developmental arc. The obligation to house the homeless moves from an individual right to a communal obligation. In the first instance, the obligation to provide housing—or the right to housing—impacts only an individual property owner's rights in his or her property. By the thirteenth century, this is a communal obligation and an undisputed component of the basic needs of the poor. We start with Mishnah Baba Metzia, chapter 8, Mishnah 6.

[Concerning the case of] one who lets a house to his fellow for
the rainy season.
He cannot remove [the lessee] from Sukkot until Pesach.
[If one lets his house] for the summer season.
[He cannot remove the lessee before the end of]
thirty days.
And [if this happens] in a large city

Whether it is the rainy season or the summer season
[He cannot remove the lessee before the end of] twelve
months.

The case described in the Mishnah is one in which a house is
rented for the winter, the rainy season. This is usually marked, in
the Land of Israel, on one side by the holiday of Sukkot, which falls
sometime in September or October, and on the other side by the
holiday of Pesach (or Passover), sometime in April. If the stipulation
of the rental agreement was that the term of the lease would be "the
rainy season," the owner could not evict the tenant prior to Pesach.
On the other hand, if the term of the lease was for the summer
season, which stretches from Pesach around to Sukkot (April to
September), the owner can evict the tenant after thirty days.

One further caveat is introduced by the Mishnah. If the rental
property was in a city, where there was high demand for housing
(think Manhattan), the lessee cannot be evicted prior to twelve
months after the agreement.

The Mishnah does not supply the reasons for the various laws
here, though they are rather suggestive. At issue, on the one hand,
is the ability of a person to make use of their property as he or she
sees fit. On the other hand, there is a need to protect the interests
of the renter. This is all the more poignant in the rainy season or in
a city where it is more difficult to find an alternative residence. The
Mishnah faces the competing demands of the renter and the owner.
The renter's claim is that there was an agreement to rent the property
for a certain period of time, and the owner had signed off on the
agreement. Additionally, the Mishnah seems to take into account
the larger reality of pain and suffering that would be endured by
the renter if they were forced to abandon their shelter during the
rainy season. This would not be the case during the summer season,
wherein living without shelter would not be as onerous.

The Mishnah is also taking into account the fact that a city
offers fewer alternatives to the displaced renter. The bottom line is
that the Mishnah recognizes that the owner's right to dispose of his
or her property is circumscribed to some extent by the right of the
renter to have shelter, especially in the rainy season. This does not
mean that the owner loses all ability to dispose of their property. In

fact, the indulgence given to the renter is limited and, at the end of
the time period, the renter is once again on the street.

The Babylonian Talmud—the commentary on the Mishnah
which was finally edited in the seventh or eighth century—raises
a different question. Why would we think that there is a difference
between the rainy season and the summer season from the point
of view of the renter? That is, just as a renter intends the whole
season when he says that he wants to rent for the rainy season, so
too would she intend the whole summer when she says that she
wishes to rent for the summer.

This question leads the Talmud to understand the Mishnah
differently. Citing R. Yehudah a mid-third-century CE Babylonian
sage, the Mishnah is now understood as follows:

> If one rents his house to his fellow without any specifications
> [of time],
> the owner cannot evict the renter from Sukkot until Pesach,
> unless he gives him thirty days notice.

This statement of R. Yehudah's is supported by a baraita, an early
authoritative statement of the same authority as the Mishnah, which
says,

> When they said thirty days and when they said twelve
> months the intention was only for the purpose of giving
> notice.

However, a differing opinion attributed to R. Asi, a Babylonian
sage who belonged to the generation before R. Yehudah, claims
that the thirty-day period of giving notice must precede the rainy
season. If even one day of the thirty days falls in the rainy season,
then the renter cannot be evicted until Pesach.

All this circumscribes what seemed to be a rather liberal
understanding of the rights of the renter. Our first reading of the
Mishnah seemed to support a robust concern for renters which
disallowed the owner of a property to evict a tenant from Sukkot
until Pesach. The Babylonian Talmud's discussion of this Mishnah
restricts the tenants' rights significantly. The owner might evict
the tenant, according to R. Yehudah, even in the midst of the rainy

season, if the owner gives thirty days notice. According to R. Asi, the notice must be given thirty days prior to the rainy season. All this leaves us with a very circumscribed right of tenancy. The law seems to be equally balanced in its concern for property rights and tenants' rights. Moreover, there is no mention of any obligation on the court or the community to provide the evicted tenant with alternative housing.

Moving Toward a Communal Obligation

As we saw above, when played out in the realm of tenant-landlord relations, the Talmud's interpretation of the Mishnah does not support a robust right to shelter at the expense of an individual's property rights. There is support for a moderate right to shelter, and a restriction on the landlord's ability to evict in certain situations. None of this yet adds up to a communal obligation to provide shelter for the homeless.

There is another tension between values which an obligation or right to housing presents. In contemporary terms, this is called "means testing." If a person shows up at a soup kitchen, do we investigate that person's actual level of resources before giving the person food? If we know, for example, that a person has a house, do we force the person to sell the house before we allow the person to benefit from the community's coffers? A Mishnah in Tractate Peah addresses this issue.

One of the questions that chapter 8 of Tractate Peah addresses is, "How much money can a person have and still be eligible for community assistance?" After deciding on a certain amount of money which would be the rabbinic equivalent of the poverty level, the Mishnah writes the following:

> [If a person is poor and needy] we do not obligate him to sell his house and his utensils [in order that he be eligible to receive money from the community].

The Mishnah is distinguishing between two different areas of need. On the one hand, a person has a need for housing. This is beyond mere shelter, as the Mishnah includes utensils in its list of assets that a person could own and still be eligible for public assistance. Although this Mishnah is not yet articulating a communal obligation to afford housing, the Mishnah is recognizing that the communal obligation to support the indigent is not impacted by owning a house and the utensils necessary to cook and so on. There is an implied recognition that a person needs both a house and the ability to support themselves in terms of food, clothing, etc. The two are not exclusive.

Before we move on to the Talmud's discussion of the communal social net, I want to look at how Maimonides in his great twelfth-century code *Mishneh Torah* codifies these laws. The interesting thing about Maimonides's codification is that he adds a moralistic voice to the law. He decides the law and then advocates for it.

In *Mishneh Torah Laws of Hiring* 6:7, Maimonides writes the following:

> He who lets a house to another for an unspecified term may not dispossess the lessee from the house unless he notifies him 30 days in advance, so as to enable him to find a place and *prevent his being thrown into the street*.
> The 30 day period is applicable only during the warm season. In the rainy season, from the Feast of Succoth to the Feast of Passover, the lessor may not dispossess the lessee (emphasis added).

Maimonides's understanding of the law combines bits of our reading of the Mishnah and some of the way that the Talmud reads the Mishnah. Maimonides agrees with R. Yehudah that the thirty-day period is for notification. On the other hand, Maimonides only allows the thirty-day period in the summer months, while in the rainy season, "the lessor may not dispossess the lessee." Maimonides claims a much more robust protection of the renter. Further, Maimonides explains his reasoning with a somewhat unusual pathos: "so as to enable him to find a place and *prevent his being thrown into the street*." It is notable that this reasoning is not found in the Talmud. Maimonides on his own makes a strong claim on the property rights of the landlord. The rights of the landlord can be circumscribed to prevent the renter being thrown into the street. This begins to sound like a right to housing or a communal obligation to provide housing.

Similarly, when codifying the law that one can qualify for communal assistance even if one owns a house and utensils, Maimonides adds pathos and a certain robustness to the communal obligation. In *Mishneh Torah Laws of Support to the Poor* chapter 9:14, Maimonides writes,

> A poor person in need of support who has a domicile and household utensils, *even if they are silver and gold,* we do not obligate him to sell his house and his utensils, but rather, he is eligible to collect, *and it is an obligation [mitzvah] to support him* (emphasis added).

The great jurist adds two significant items here. First, he qualifies the household utensils: "even if they are silver and gold" we still don't obligate him to sell them in order to receive support from the community. This is something that is not mentioned in the Babylonian Talmud's discussion of the Mishnah.[1] Maimonides's decision enshrines the idea that not only is a person entitled to a house, a person is entitled to a home. These utensils which make up the person's space are not accounted for or assessed against the person's eligibility to draw from the communal welfare fund.

Then, Maimonides reinforces this first move by saying that it is a *mitzvah* or an obligation to support him. Maimonides is stating unequivocally that this support is not beyond the letter of the law, but is the law itself. The community is obligated to support this person who is poor and needy despite the fact that the person owns a home.

We are moving toward a recognition of housing as part of a community's obligations to its residents.

The Obligations of Citizenship

In chapter 1, we discussed part of the third-century CE Mishnah Baba Bathra 1:5, focusing on the question of tenants in common building a gatehouse. That Mishnah continues with a discussion of the residents of a town having to contribute toward the town's infrastructure.

> They may coerce one to [participate in the] building of a wall, a double door and bolt for the city.
> Rabban Shimon ben Gamliel says, Not all cities need a wall.

The debate between the anonymous voice of the first line, and the dissenting voice of Rabban Shimon ben Gamliel, is about public policy. Is a wall, a double door, and a bolt necessary for all cities or only cities that have special circumstances, perhaps border cities or cities plagued by highway bandits? Rabban Shimon ben Gamliel's argument seemingly would be that a resident of a city cannot be forced to contribute to a merely decorative wall which would serve no purpose. If the town council decided that it was unbecoming for our town not to have a wall, that would not necessarily be enough of a warrant to justify forcing residents to contribute to the building of the wall.

The Mishnah then continues with a short discussion of what constitutes residency in a town.

> How long must one be in the city and be [considered] as a resident? Twelve months.
> If one bought a lodging, behold one is [considered] as a resident immediately.

This Mishnah then articulates a basic claim about what a city is. A city is a community of obligation. Residency in a city is determined by the point at which people assume the obligations of the city. This Mishnah states that the requirement for residency is twelve months. At the end of that time, one is obligated to contribute to the security fund or the infrastructure fund. To translate this into a contemporary idiom: after twelve months, one is taxed as a resident to help fulfill the obligations of residency.

This conception of residency runs counter to a contemporary American conception wherein the privileges of citizenship are conferred after a certain amount of time. The Mishnah's conception of residency differs. The resident is one who joins a community of obligation. After a residency requirement, one assumes those obligations along with the rest of the community.

The discussion of this Mishnah in the seventh-century Babylonian Talmud introduces a more robust understanding of the obligations of residency.

> At thirty days [one is assessed for] the soup-kitchen, at three months—the welfare fund, at six months—the clothing fund, at nine—the burial fund, at twelve—the city's infrastructure (Baba Bathra 8a).

According to this source, a person is considered a resident at different times for different obligations. At thirty days, one is taxed for the soup kitchen, at six months the clothing fund, etc. An interesting thing about this assessment is again the way in which it is counterintuitive to the American experience. There is no term of residency required in order to eat from the soup kitchen. In fact, the discussion in the Mishnah (Pe'ah 8:7)[2] takes the opposite tack. The question there is about what the community is obligated to provide for a poor person wandering from town to town, who is not a resident of this town.

> [The town] cannot supply a poor person wandering from place to place, less than one loaf of bread [which can last for two meals].[3] If he stays the night in the town, they provide him with the necessities for sleeping. If he will be staying over Shabbat, they provide him with three meals.

This is all to reinforce the point that the requirement of residency is the assumption of the obligations of the city. There is no residency requirement in order to draw on the resources of the city. This last Mishnah we cited, however, seems to invoke the obligation of providing shelter. The ambiguous phrase "necessities for sleeping"/parnassat linah[4] might imply shelter. The Babylonian Talmud, however, cites Rav Papa, a fourth-century Babylonian sage, who asks, "What is parnassat linah?" and answers, "a bed and a pillow."

The Talmud, in the continuation of its discussion of the collection of the tax for welfare, raises another question. Is the money that is raised for the soup kitchen, for example, fungible? Can it be used for the clothing fund? Or can it even be used for general community needs not connected to the poor, such as repairing the synagogue, etc.? The Talmud quotes an early source (a baraita):

> The people of the town are permitted to make the welfare fund into a soup-kitchen fund, or a soup-kitchen fund into a welfare fund, and to change the purpose of the money for whatever they want.[5]

This statement starts off simply saying that the money collected for the poor is fungible. If there is not enough money in the soup kitchen fund and too much in the welfare fund, the welfare fund money can "repurposed." The dodgy piece here is the last phrase: "to change the purpose of the money for whatever they want." What exactly is the scope of "whatever they want"? Does this include only expenses related to the poor, or does this include anything the community wants, from repairing the community center roof to sending the rabbi on vacation? There is a dispute about this. For our purposes, the interesting answer is provided by the thirteenth-century Andalusian sage Nachmanides. He quotes an earlier Spanish sage, Rabbi Yosef ibn Migash (1077–1141):

> R. Yosef Halevi ibn Migash OBM explained [the phrase in the Talmud "for whatever they want"] that it was specifically for the needs of the poor such as housing, clothing, and sleeping needs [i.e., bedding], however, other [communal] needs, and even for the purpose of fulfilling a commandment, no [i.e., you cannot use the money for that].

R. ibn Migash strongly states that "for whatever they want" refers specifically to the needs of the poor and not the general needs of the community.[6] Independently, another Spanish sage of relatively the same time period as Nachmanides, Rabbi Meir Halevi Abulafiah (1170–1244), says that the money might be used for such things as "clothing, housing and sleeping needs" but not for general community needs, since that would be stealing from the poor.[7] In other words, Abulafia would argue that the money already belongs to the poor once it is collected, and therefore, the community can only direct it to fulfilling the needs of the poor.

Here for the first time is an explicit statement that housing is a need of the poor which the community is obligated to provide. It is one of the legitimate uses that can be made of the money collected for the poor. Significantly, once housing is added to the list of "needs of the poor," there is no one who objects to this. No one claims that the community need not provide shelter. This, I think, is important. It points to the fact that there was an implied obligation to provide housing for the poor, and an implied acknowledgment that housing was a necessity. We saw this in one form or another in the discussions of eviction and eligibility to collect money from the community fund. I want to suggest then, that once someone articulated housing as a need of the poor, it caused a certain jolt of recognition, an "Aha!" moment, a moment of saying, "Of course." This goes back, to my mind, to Isaiah "to provide the poor wanderer with shelter." This idea was part of the general conceptual and moral world of the rabbis, even though it was not articulated explicitly, and perhaps only lived underground. However, when it was finally articulated, there was a general acceptance of the notion.

We see then, the development of the need of housing for the homeless from out of Isaiah's nascent plea, to a factor in landlord-tenant relationships, to a consideration in deciding on one's status as poor or needy, to an obligation on the community.

The Implications of Homelessness[8]

Homelessness is an issue that raises deep emotions. Homelessness strikes at the heart of what our conception of our cities is, and even what our own home is. The language that is and has been used to describe both the phenomenon of homelessness and homeless people themselves lays bare the conflicted feelings that people have around the issue. On the one hand, most people have feelings of sympathy toward those who are destitute—and none are so destitute as those that cannot even manage to put a roof over their or their children's heads. On the other hand, the homeless impinge on my sense of myself. They are not someplace else, although they don't belong anywhere. There are many mechanisms with which we negotiate this tension. We talk about the "deserving poor" as opposed to frauds or fakes or scam artists who, it is claimed, actually live fine lives on the basis of the donations that they extort from us through emotional appeal. We all would like to help the deserving poor, but not give money to the undeserving poor, the homeless people who would go and spend the money on alcohol or drugs.

We talk about vagrancy and slothfulness. The fact that homeless people live, literally, nowhere, challenges and perhaps threatens the efforts I put into living somewhere. Why should I have to be faced with a "bum" (to recall an anachronism from my youth) who needs a shower on my way home from a hard day at the office? What right does some stranger have to inflict his suffering (which is not my fault) on me? I pay taxes. *Somebody* should take care of this.

There is a deep need to distance myself from homeless people since, especially in the urban areas that I have been discussing, being homeless is the nightmare of all of us in homes. Being reminded that the distance between "homed" and "homeless" can be rather short is a frightening prospect.

At the same time, and for this very reason, the homeless person whom I encounter on the street is the paradigmatic Other, the Stranger to whom I must respond. It is in the face of the homeless stranger that I can encounter the depth of need and suffering which should only brook one answer: *hineni*, "here I am." It is the homeless stranger whose face points me also beyond herself to all the Strangers who are in need, who should join this conversation about justice as equals—as residents of this city and community with a voice, a commanding voice that I must hear and respond to.

Homelessness strikes at the heart of the community of obligation. Being part of a community involves being somewhere. Being homeless is literally being nowhere. Having no address, having no home, brings in its wake having no community. If people come to populate cities in order to, in some way, pool resources for added security and shelter, homeless people are not city dwellers. For them, the city is another wilderness—a wilderness which threatens to overtake the rest of the city ethically.

The web of relations that is the community is threatened by the Other who is not actually threatening; the Other who is unseen and unheard and therefore not part of the conversation. For the relationships of response—seeing the face of the Other and recognizing in it the need that must be responded to—that comprise the community of obligation; for those relationships to work, to effectively be just, I must be able to engage the Other face-to-face. In our large, anonymous megalopolises I must at least be able to see in the face of another person the need that points beyond this specific relationship toward the many other Strangers—persons in need, hungry persons, suffering, poor people—beyond my response to just this one person. All the Others, the Strangers, must be able to enter this relationship—as equals—in order to create a just city. While I don't have an absolute obligation for all the poor and suffering people, I do have a proportional obligation to respond.[9] My proportional obligation is mediated by the polis, the institutions of the city which are, or should be, the institutions of justice. This is how the community of obligation should look.

However, homelessness is a material affliction which carries with it a greater danger—the danger of disappearance. If the city does not have enough places to house the homeless and yet criminalizes vagrancy, sleeping on the sidewalk, even distributing food on the street—the homeless then are defined not as Other but as non-Other, that is, as nonexistent. To criminalize homelessness is to refuse to see the people in our cities who are nowhere. In criminalizing homelessness, we are refusing to look into the face of people who would and should command a just response from us. If, however, instead of responding, I define them into nonexistence before the law, I have obviated the possibility of response.

Changing the Conversation

There has been a growing international movement beginning with the Universal Declaration of Human Rights in 1948 to recognize the right to housing as a basic human right. This right has been reaffirmed since then in many subsequent conferences and covenants.[10]

The issue has not however been settled. The United States, among others, has not recognized the right to housing. Moreover, the housing crisis in the United States has gone from bad to worse in many areas. In Los Angeles, the city in which I live, there are more homeless people (over sixty thousand according to the 2007 LAHSA study) than the total populations of many cities. Over the course of a year, more than a hundred thousand people are homeless in Los Angeles, according to the same study.[11]

According to a very recent study,

> The housing and homelessness situation in the United States has worsened over the past two years, particularly due to the current economic and foreclosure crises. ... The Sarasota, Florida, Herald Tribune noted that, by some estimates, more than 311,000 tenants nationwide have been evicted from homes this year after lenders took over the properties. ...
>
> In Denver, nearly 30% of the homeless population is newly homeless. ... The State of Massachusetts reports that the number of families living in shelters has risen by 33% in the past year. In Atlanta, Georgia, the Metro Atlanta Task Force for the Homeless reports that 30% of all people coming into the Day Services Center daily are newly homeless. In Concord, New Hampshire, the food pantry at First Congregational Church serves about 4,000 meals to over 800 people each month, around double the rate from 2007.
>
> Of the 25 cities surveyed by the US Conference of Mayors for its annual Hunger and Homelessness Report, 19 reported an increase in homelessness in 2008. On average, cities reported a 12 percent increase.[12]

This report documents the disturbing fact that many of our large metropolitan areas are spending much more money on criminalizing the homeless than on services for the homeless.[13]

Recognizing that providing housing to the homeless is a communal obligation, an obligation that the polis needs to fulfill, rather than a right that the individual must demand, changes the conversation about the issue. As part of the larger picture of the city as a community of obligation, this further articulation of the web of responsibilities and commitments that residents have to each other, mediated and facilitated by governmental institutions, the obligation to provide housing moves the burden of proof from those who have no shelter to those who must provide it. The language of communal obligation allows us to think about how we as a city are or are not fulfilling our obligations to the residents of our city—to those among us with whom we are in a web of often anonymous relationships and toward whom we must respond.

From Rant to Action

In chapter 1 of the Book of Isaiah, we find the following:

17   Learn to do good. Devote yourselves to justice; Aid the wronged. Uphold the rights of the orphan; Defend the cause of the widow.
     [...]
20   But if you refuse and disobey, You will be devoured by the sword. —For it was the LORD who spoke.
21   Alas, she has become a harlot, The faithful city That was filled with justice, Where righteousness dwelt—But now murderers.

In the first recorded speech in the biblical book which bears his name, Isaiah takes Israel to task for bringing sacrifices while ignoring the plight of the poor and the widow. In verse 17, Isaiah, channeling God, offers an olive branch as it were. If you, the Israelites, do justice, I, God, will erase your sins and you will prosper. If however you "refuse and disobey," things will not go so well. "You will be devoured by the sword." Verse 21 is the beginning of a coda in which Isaiah catalogues the current ills of Israel. The people who were great and good are no longer either great or good.

Is there any practical impact to these verses for the contemporary Jewish community? When Isaiah says "Learn to do good" or "Devote yourselves to justice," how does one cash this out? What do I have to do today? In order for this to mean anything real in our lives, we have to answer the questions: Where? When? How much? To whom?

These are the questions of the jurist. The jurist par excellence, Maimonides, quotes this chapter in a very interesting and practical way.

> On fast days [Jews] distribute food to the poor. Any fast day
> on which the people ate and rested and did not distribute
> charity to the poor, behold they are akin to murderers. About
> them it is stated in the tradition "Righteousness would rest
> there, but now only murderers" (Maimonides, *Mishneh Torah,*
> *Laws of Support to the Poor, 9:4*).

Maimonides reads Isaiah's hyperbolic oratory: "righteousness
would rest there, but now only murderers," and asks "what exactly
do you mean by that?" His answer (based in part on the Babylonian
Talmud Sanhedrin 32a) is that when you perform righteousness in
the form of fasting, yet you ignore the real existential needs of the
poor, you are not righteous—you are akin to murderers.[14] Therefore, according to Maimonides, what Isaiah means specifically is
that on fast days, money must be distributed to the poor. The exhortation is then assimilated into the legal system and deployed in
a very specific way.

Walking the Talk

I want to suggest that there are two levels on which one
should act—the personal and the political. The personal level is the
obligation to treat homeless people we come across as members of
our community. Giving a panhandler a dollar or lunch is not going to
fix the political problem; why is there homelessness in this affluent
society? However, giving a homeless person a dollar while stopping
to talk to him is an act that begins to erase the boundaries between
the housed and the homeless. The simple act of giving money,
a bottle of water, or a sandwich to a homeless person, and stopping
for a minute to chat, affects the giver as much as the recipient.
Contact has been made across the barrier that is supposed to divide
between us and them. Face-to-face, I can now see and hear the need
and the vulnerability of those who sleep on the streets of my city.

The second level is political action. In different cities, the
tactics may be different. However, the goal must be to have enough
affordable housing stock so that nobody has to live on the street. The
goal is to have enough affordable housing stock and the support in
place for people to be able to transition to homes, so that people

can live with their human dignity intact. I am not arguing for a shelter bed. I am arguing that if we are to ever be able to call our cities places where righteousness dwells, we must work toward the possibility of housing for everybody. There are many different ways to get from here to there: inclusionary zoning, low-income housing, housing vouchers. Different solutions will fit different cities. Many smart people are working on specific solutions. The goal of those solutions needs to be kept in mind. We cannot consider ourselves a righteous city when thousands of people live on the streets.

Notes

[1]   Moreover, the Palestinian Talmud, which does mention the quality of the utensils, goes in the opposite direction. The Palestinian Talmud writes that if a person is using gold utensils, we force him to sell them and use silver utensils, if silver then stone, etc. In this light, Maimonides's statement is even stronger.

[2]   Quoted further on in the discussion in Baba Bathra (9a).

[3]   This is Rashi's gloss on the technical definition which the Mishnah supplies which is "a loaf that costs a *pundiyon* when the monetary exchange rate is four *seah* to a *sela*."

[4]   Danby retains the ambiguity of the Hebrew by translating "what is needful to support him for the night."

[5]   Baba Bathra 8b.

[6]   On the dispute here between ibn Megash and Maimonides, see Mark R. Cohen, *Poverty and Charity in the Jewish Community of Medieval Egypt*, 219.

[7]   Rabbi Meir Halevi Abulafia, *Sefer Yad Ramah* to Baba Bathra 17b sec. 90.

[8]   The thinking in this section is dependent on Emmanuel Levinas, *Totality and Infinity: An Essay on Exteriority*, trans by Alphonso Lingis (Pittsburgh, PA: Duquesne University Press, 1969) 212–214; Annabelle Herzog, "Is Liberalism All We Need? Lévinas's *Politics of Surplus, Political Theory* vol. 30 no. 2, April 2002, 204–227; and Kathleen R. Arnold, *Homelessness, Citizenship, and Identity: The Uncanniness of Late Modernity*.

[9]   Agreeing with Kwame Anthony Appiah's argument in his book *Cosmopolitanism: Ethics in a World of Strangers* (W. W. Norton, 2006).

[10]   Convention for the Elimination of all forms of Racial Discrimination (1969); International Bill of Rights, International Covenant of Economic, Social and Cultural Rights (1976); International Covenant of Civil and Political Rights (1976); Habitat II (1996).

[11]   *2007 Greater Los Angeles Homeless Count: Sponsored by Los Angeles Homeless Services Authority*, pp. 17–18.

[12]   *Homes Not Handcuffs: The Criminalization of Homelessness in U.S. Cities: A Report by the National Law Center on Homelessness & Poverty and the National Coalition for the Homeless*, July 2009, pp. 17–18.

[13]   This refers to cities that "do not provide enough affordable housing, shelter space, and food to meet the need," yet they "use the criminal justice system to punish people living on the street for doing things that they need to do to survive." They do this by enacting measures to "prohibit activities such as sleeping/camping, eating, sitting, and/or begging in public spaces and include criminal penalties for violation of these laws. Some cities have even enacted food-sharing restrictions that punish groups and individuals for serving homeless people" (*Homes Not Handcuffs*, p. 14). Los Angeles was ranked number 1, as the "meanest city" in the nation (*Homes Not Handcuffs*, p. 33).

[14]   This is especially so if there was a regular distribution of food on which the poor depended. If that distribution was disrupted by the fast day, the poor would go hungry. Cf. Babylonian Talmud Tractate Sanhedrin 35a and the commentaries of Rashi and Rabbi Menahem HaMeiri.

Chapter 6

Labor

Labor is at the heart of the web of relations which makes up the community of obligation. Whether one is an employer or an employee or whether one benefits from someone else's labor as a consumer, labor is a central connective tissue of the urban spaces in which we live. Oftentimes the only connection between different parts of Los Angeles—the megalopolis which I call home—is the fact that the person who cleans one's home or takes care of one's children comes from the other side of town. Or conversely, that one leaves one's own children in the care of a relative in order to traverse the economic and geographic divide between east and west and care for someone else's children.

What is labor in Rabbinic Judaism? How are we to think about work and workers? What are the obligations of employers and employees to each other?

My Servants and Not Servants of Servants

One of the bright lines when thinking about labor is the line between slave labor and wage labor. What are the larger implications of this difference?

Rav, a sage who lived in Babylonia in the fourth century and was one of the founders of the Babylonian Rabbinic Academies, said the following:

> A worker may back out of [his work commitment] even in the middle of the [work] day, . . . for it is written [in Scripture] "For unto Me the children of Israel are servants; they are My servants" and not servants of servants (Babylonian Talmud Baba Metzia 10a).

Rav is pushing hard on a verse in Leviticus in order to arrive at his interpretation or midrash. The verse in full reads as follows:

> For it is to Me that the Israelites are servants: they are My servants, whom I freed from the land of Egypt, I the LORD your God (Lev. 25:55).

The verse is the tagline, as it were, to a set of laws referring to an Israelite who falls on bad times and is forced to sell himself into slavery to a non-Israelite. The laws clarify the mechanisms by which that Israelite can be redeemed from slavery. The set of laws (Lev. 25:47–54) ends with our verse.

Rav reads our verse very closely, as a verse unto itself. He presses on the statement, "It is to Me that the Israelites are servants." The continuation of the verse already narrates that God freed the Israelites from slavery in Egypt. What might the purpose of this first half of the verse be? Rav says that the implication of the verse is the Israelites are *only* servants to God—and not servants to other people, who are also servants of God. This is a rather radical statement. Following the logic of this statement, slavery would be abolished in total. We know, unfortunately, that this wasn't the case. However, the implication for workers is similarly radical. Rav's interpretive logic leads him to say that the end result of this statement is that workers cannot be bound to a labor contract against their will—and that, even in the middle of a work day, they may walk off the job.

Follow the Way of the Good

What then is signified by the labor contract? What is being bought by wages? What is being paid for? There is an interesting story later on in Tractate Baba Metzia of the Babylonian Talmud which highlights these issues:

> There were porters who broke a barrel of wine belonging to
> Rabbah bar bar Hana, [while in his service].
> And he took their garments [for the damage caused];
> and they came and complained before Rav.
> He said to [Rabbah bar bar Hana]: "Return their garments!"
> The latter questioned him: Is this the law?

> He answered: Yes, [as it is written]: "So follow the way of the
> good" (Prov. 2:20).
> [Rabbah bar bar Hana] returned their garments.
> [The porters] said: "We are poor, we were working the whole
> day, we are hungry and have nothing [to eat]."
> [Rav] said to [Rabbah]: "Pay them their wages."
> [Rabbah] asked [again]: "Is this the law?"
> He answered: "Yes; as it is written: 'And keep to the paths of
> the just'" (Prov. 2:20).

This story describes a situation of a good relationship gone bad. Initially, Rabbah bar bar Hana hired men to carry a barrel of wine from one place to another. We might assume that he was going to pay them an appropriate wage since he is an upstanding sage and knows the law. Something untoward happens and the barrel breaks. We can assume that this was not the result of negligence since that eventuality is covered by the law, and in that case, the workers would be liable. So an accident happens and the wine barrel is broken and the wine is lost. Rabbah is miffed. Not only is his wine not where he wanted it to be, his wine is lost. He demands payment from the workers. As a surety—or perhaps as a down payment—he seizes the coats off their backs.

Rav, the head of one of the two main Babylonian academies and one of the pair of sages credited with founding the rabbinic movement in Babylonia, acting as a judge, orders Rabbah bar bar Hana to return the garments and to pay the hungry and impoverished workers their wages. At each order, Rabbah demands to know if Rav is handing down a legal decision—whether he is acting in his capacity as a judge or speaking in another capacity— as a moral leader. The implication seems to be that if this is the law, Rabbah will follow it. However, if it is merely a suggestion of supererogatory behavior, Rabbah would not feel the same level of obligation to follow the ruling.

Rav's reply is itself fascinating. He claims that his decision is the law. However, the prooftext that he cites to ground his decision is not a legal text per se. He cites a verse from Proverbs which is arguing for a practice of righteousness—not a verse which anchors any specific legal action.

There are two possibilities for interpreting Rav's statement. Either he is saying that returning the garments is the law because one should act in a righteous manner, or that acting in a righteous manner is itself the law.

In either case, one can now ask after the implications of this exchange for the discussion about labor. Are we to think that the employment contract is not about paying for specific work to be done, but rather agreeing to pay a worker such that he can eat and in exchange the worker will work for the employer? It is not the value added to a product or the specific goals of the labor (i.e., that the vat is moved from here to there) that is contracted for. Rather the contract is for labor itself, and the payment is so that the worker can eat.

This, however, cannot be the case, can it? Do I not have a reasonable expectation as an employer that when I hire somebody to mow my lawn or assist in making my widget, that they will in fact do what they are hired to do? However, on the other hand, as an employee, do I not have a right to expect that if I work for a whole day in the honest expectation that I will be accomplishing an agreed-upon task, that I will finish the day with the ability to, at the least, feed myself? This story insists that labor contracts are not that simple, that actually the worker-employer relationship cannot be reduced to the production of a good or a value added; that the web of relationships which comprise the community of obligation also encompasses the relationship of the labor contract.

Our Talmudic story also demonstrates one of the ways in which the hortatory—here, the prophetic demand for righteous behavior—might be translated into the prescriptive—the legal demand that the worker be paid for his work even in the case when the work was not "good."

The relationship of worker and employer, and the discourse of economic justice, are not easy. There are expectations and obligations. Just as there is a bright line between wage labor and slave labor, there is a similar line between paid labor and charity. The community is obligated to support those who are indigent. An employer contracts with a worker to perform a task and pays him for it. It is the complicated nature of this relationship which must be worked out.

Indeed, some of these complications are worked out in Mishnah Baba Metzia (chapter 6 in the Mishnah), and subsequently in the Babylonian Talmud's discussion of these texts.

"Do Not Withhold Good from Those to Whom It Is Due"

The labor relationship, the relationship between worker and employer, is a complicated one to conceptualize within the community of obligation. On the one hand, the relationship between employer and worker should be similar to any other relationship with another person in the city. This means that it is a relationship which is based on obligation. Coming face-to-face with any other person, I am struck by their need and respond to that need. The relationship that is thus created is asymmetrical. It is a relationship in which there is no expectation of mutuality, a relationship in which my response to you is not in any way predicated on your subsequently responding to me.

On the other hand, the labor relationship is one in which the employer pays for work or work time. The relationship of employment, almost by definition, is not one of responding to the needs of the other person but using the other person — the worker — to fulfill a task. At the same time, the relationship of the worker to the employer is also utilitarian — labor in exchange for compensation.

Within the rabbinic community of obligation, work itself is not a problem. Work is often spoken of in laudatory terms. According to some sages, there is a commandment to work six days a week just as there is a commandment to rest on the seventh.[1] There are statements attributed to various Talmudic sages which praise all work as honoring the one who does it.[2] Work itself is not a problem.[3]

As stated above, the problem is the relationship between the worker and her employer. In order to understand this relationship better and how the demands for economic justice fit into the larger context of the community of obligation, it would be helpful to explore the way in which labor is contextualized in rabbinic literature. What is the conceptual world within which the labor relationship is embedded? To this end, we look at a Mishnah and the commentary of the Palestinian and Babylonian Talmuds at the beginning of the sixth chapter of Baba Metzia.

Mishnah Baba Metzia 6:1 states the following:

> One who hires workers, and they defraud one another, their only recourse is indignation.

This statement leaves two glaring questions. The first is, "What does it mean that they "defrauded one another?" What was the fraud? The second question is of course what is the practical ramification of "indignation"? One might correctly translate the Hebrew word *tar'omet* more strongly: anger, rage, shouting. However, this still leaves open the question of what, if anything, does this accomplish legally for the aggrieved party?

The first question is addressed by both Talmuds. The Palestinian Talmud[4] understands that an employer could defraud the workers by lying to them about what the prevailing wages are. According to the Talmud, a potential employer offers work to job seekers. They ask the employer: "How much do workers normally get paid?" The employer says, "Most get $5 an hour." In actuality, most get $10 an hour. However, since the workers agree to work for $5 an hour, there is no effective remedy, and they are only left with indignation/*tar'omet*.

The workers could defraud the employer in a similar manner. The employer asks what most people earn. The workers say $10 an hour, although in actuality, most people earn $5 an hour. The employer agrees to the $10 an hour and when he discovers that he has been intentionally misinformed, his only recourse (since he *has* actually agreed to the terms) is indignation/*tar'omet*.

A striking aspect of this is that "indignation" is seen as, in some way, a legal remedy. That is, it is the answer of the court. The court essentially says, "I have no justification to compensate you monetarily. However, I support your claim of having been wronged and affirm the legitimacy of your outrage." I would suggest that this is a coherent ruling only in a context which recognizes that righteousness is important. Another way to think of this is that in a two-tiered system in which the full measure of justice is not necessarily meted out by the courts but in the "higher" realm of divine justice—where it is not necessarily assumed that the courts can always reach a totally just outcome—especially in the realm of punishment or compensation; where that divine realm is understood and treated as equally as important as the human realm of the courts; in this type of system, acknowledging the legitimacy of one party's righteous rage is a very powerful statement. (Let us bracket, for the moment, the question of whether this system might have a contemporary analogue without the divine.)

I turn now to the Babylonian Talmud, and want to tarry for a few moments in this relatively lengthy discussion.

The Babylonian Talmud initially proposes that the phrase "they defraud one another" refers to workers defrauding each other—as opposed to the Palestinian Talmud's understanding that it is the workers and the employer who are defrauding each other. What would this look like? The Talmud tries several different options for understanding how this might be imagined. One way of picturing this, the Talmud explains, is that the employer sends one worker out to hire other workers. The first worker, the employer's agent, is told by the employer to hire workers at $4 an hour. He offers $3 an hour. The workers agree to work for $3 an hour. This, however, cannot be a case of indignation. The Talmud points out that the workers actually agreed to the terms. They had no idea at that time that the employer had authorized his agent to offer them more so when they accepted the offer of $3 an hour; it was a wholehearted acceptance. There is then no basis for indignation.

At a later point in the discussion, the Talmud questions this logic. It is true, the Talmud argues, that the workers agreed to the $3 an hour and, at that time, the agreement was wholehearted since they did not know that the employer had offered $4 an hour. However, once they found out that the agent could have offered them more for their labor they confront him with the following admonition from Proverbs (3:27): "Do not withhold good from those to whom it is due, [when it is in your power to do it]." The Talmud seems to be assuming that there is an obligation (moral but perhaps not legal) upon the agent to keep in mind the material benefit of the workers and not only his employer. The introduction of this verse fills the indignation with content. There is an assumption of righteousness in which one will not deprive a person of a benefit which is morally due them. While this is not a rule of the market, it is a principle of a community which aspires to right conduct.

This move in the text might afford us the ability to rethink the worker-employer relationship. Rather than a relationship which by definition is utilitarian and market based, in which my sole interest as an employer is to get some added value for my product which I am willing to pay for, the relationship has the potential to be one in which the employer is also responding to the need of the worker. In her engagement with the worker, the employer responds to the worker's needs and is not merely buying labor as a commodity.

What Is Labor Worth?

At one point in this discussion, the possibility is raised that the fraud was perpetrated by the agent offering $4 an hour when the owner had said $3 an hour. An objection is proffered. There would be no problem if the agent states that he himself guarantees the salary ("Your wages are on me.") In that case, we force the agent to pay the extra dollar and, again, there would be no reason for indignation. However, if the agent says, "Your wages are on the employer," i.e., he does not set himself up as some manner of subcontractor but rather as a person merely fulfilling the word of the employer, then the legal situation is more complicated. On the one hand, the agent does not have the right to change the terms that the owner had set— and the agent himself did not accept responsibility for the salaries of the workers. On the other hand, the workers accepted the work at $4 an hour.

The Talmud then suggests that the solution might be as easy as going outside and seeing how much workers are actually getting paid. This suggestion is countered by the possibility that the situation is one in which some workers get paid three and some workers get paid four, and the workers tell the owner, "If you had not offered us four, we would have searched and found employment at four." There is a dispute among the commentaries in understanding what to make of the fact that some workers are making $3 an hour and some are making $4 an hour. Rabbi Yitzhak Alfasi (eleventh-century North Africa and Spain) says that there is work that is worth $3 an hour, and there is work that is worth $4 an hour. When there are workers getting paid three and others getting paid four, it is because the former are doing work worth three and the latter are doing work worth one more. The workers, in this interpretation, are saying, "If you had said that you only wanted $3-an-hour work, we would have found an employer who wanted $4-an-hour work."

Rashi (Rabbi Shlomo Yitzhaki, eleventh–twelfth century France) interprets this differently. He says that the text is talking about the same work all the time. The only variable is what the worker can get for his work, or what the market will bear. The workers, in this interpretation, are saying, "If we had known that you were only paying $3 an hour, we would have found an employer who was in greater need of workers and would therefore have paid us $4 an hour."

In this dispute, Alfasi understands work as a commodity — that is, as a thing that can be bought and sold. All labor has a price tag. Workers, by this logic, are paid to deliver labor. According to Rashi, the relationship is more fluid. Work does not have a price tag per se, rather a labor situation has a price tag. That price is dependent on the situation of the worker and the employer.

Rashi's understanding of the labor relationship opens the possibility that a worker's work is not being bought by the employer. Rather, the worker is being paid so that he can work. The difference is whether or not an employer must take into account situations or context which are not immediately related to the performance of a specific task. Some of these are closely related, though not necessarily included in a description of the work or task at hand. These would include meals, water breaks, rest, etc. Some are more peripherally related to the job at hand and more closely related to the worker as a person. This is what we call "benefits" in contemporary society — health care, pension, etc. The logic behind the inclusion of benefits is that work is not a commodity like bricks, and therefore, it must be treated within a social and not merely an economic context.

The Custom of the Place / Minhag Hamedinah

The Mishnah and the Talmud recognize another consideration which intervenes in the labor relationship, reinforcing the idea that the arrangements between worker and employer are not a private matter. Mishnah Baba Metzia 7:1 reads as follows:

> One who hires workers and demands that they arrive early and leave late.
> In a place where it was customary that they did not arrive early and leave late, he cannot force them.
> In a place where it is customary to feed one's workers. He must feed them.
> [Where it is customary] to supply them with sweets, he must supply them.
> Everything is according to the custom of the place.

This Mishnah lays out an extra set of work rules. It assumes that the workday is defined by the practice of a specific locale. If in a given area, the workday is dawn to dusk, an employer cannot demand that workers begin work earlier or end later. The Mishnah goes further and says that even if the employer explicitly said at the time that he hired the workers that he expects them to come in earlier and leave later—he is not allowed to abrogate the custom of the place. If in that place workers do not come in earlier, then the employer cannot force them to do so. The same is true for meals and even "sweets" at the workplace. If the labor contract is understood in a city to mean that the employer will feed his workers, then he does not have the right not to feed them, or even to contract not to feed them.

The Babylonian Talmud (Baba Metzia 83a–b) goes one step further in this direction. The Mishnah is challenged on the grounds that this law (that the custom of the place dictates) is so obvious that it should not need stating. The Talmud answers that the Mishnah also refers to a situation where an employer is paying his workers more than the prevailing wage. One might have thought that in that situation, the employer could claim that he had the right to demand that the workers come in earlier and leave later. Or the employer could claim that he only paid more because he was expecting the workers to come in earlier and leave later. This is the reason that this Mishnah needs stating, the Talmud concludes. Even in a case where the employer claims against the workers that he had intended his higher salary so that they would work a longer day, they can reply, "We understood that the higher remuneration is only for better work but not longer hours." In short, an employer cannot unilaterally override the custom of the place—even if the custom of a specific place contradicts the law of another place.

As if to reinforce this earlier interpretation, the Babylonian Talmud, later in the same chapter (86a), interrogates the Mishnah's use of the word "everything" in the phrase: "Everything is according to the custom of the territory."

> What does "everything" include?
> It includes a place in which it is customary to eat a meal and drink wine and then go to the field.
> For if he says to them: 'Come early and bring [food] for yourself.' They can say to him: 'You are not the source of everything.'

The Talmudic understanding of the custom of the place is that it is a robust concept which can stand up to the onslaught of an employer who wishes to trample it. The custom of the place is a source of authority for the regulation of the labor situation whereas the employer is not. This is a serious and conscious impingement on the authority of the market.

The Residents of the Town / Bnei Ha-ir

The Talmudic discussion of worker justice starts at two different points. We have discussed one of these points which is the distinction between work and slavery or workers and slaves. With the concept of "the custom of the place," we have just begun discussing the second point which is that although a labor contract might be negotiated between two parties—the worker and the employer—and the work relationship might seem to only involve those two parties, it is not actually a case of private contracting. The community has an interest in, and is a party to, the labor relationship.

This is articulated in a number of different ways. In the conversation concerning the community's responsibilities to its residents (noted above) in Tractate Baba Bathra (8b) of the Babylonian Talmud, a baraita, a Tannaitic text, is cited.

> The "residents of a town" are permitted to set parameters
> for weights, for prices and for workers' wages, and to punish
> those who abrogate their ordinances.

The "residents of a town" (*bnei ha'ir*) are either some sort of representative body of residents, or some sort of elected council or actually all the people of the town (and sometimes all the members of a certain guild). What is clear is that they do have the right to intervene in the market (setting wage and price caps or floors) and to enforce their rulings. There is a dispute about whether they can set a ceiling or a floor for wages. It is not however in dispute that they can intervene. In other words, the relationship between worker and employer is open to legal intervention and supervision by the polis, the city.

An example of the (complicated) power to enforce labor conditions is cited on the following folio:

> Two tanners came to an agreement with each other
> that if one works on his fellow's day, his hide is torn.
> One went and worked on his fellow's day.
> [The other one] tore his hide.
> They came before Rava.
> Rava obligated him to pay.
> Rav Yeimar bar Shlamya asked of Rava: [What of] "to punish
> those who abrogate their ordinances?"
> Rava did not answer him.
> Rav Papa said: He acted appropriately in not answering him.
> This [the baraita's ruling] is referring to a case where there is
> no "important person."
> But where there is an "important person," not everyone like
> him can reach a binding agreement.

In this case, the two tanners agreed to certain work rules which included sanctions for breaking the rules. One of the tanners broke the rules and the sanction was enforced by the other tanner. The case was then brought before Rava (fourth-century Babylonian sage). The tanner whose hide had been destroyed obviously wanted to question the legitimacy of the sanction, but more than that, the appeal to Rava questioned the ability of workers to draw up binding agreements and to enforce them. Both of these issues were addressed in the exchange that followed.

Rava first obligated the tanner who had enforced the sanction (i.e., had destroyed the other tanner's work) to pay damages. Rav Yeimar, a younger colleague or a student of Rava's, challenges Rava with the baraita that we cited above, which mandated that the residents of a city might "punish those who abrogate their ordinances." Rav Yeimar is obviously assuming that the agreement between the two tanners fell into the category of the residents of a town intervening in the market, a practice that was legitimated by the earlier ruling.

Rava ignored Rav Yeimar's challenge. Another student of Rava's, Rav Papa, applauds Rava's silence. He understands Rava's "brush off" of Rav Yeimar as being completely appropriate since the earlier ruling does not apply in the case of the tanners. This is because the earlier ruling is only in a case where there is no "important person." However, in a situation or place in which there is an important person, there is no ability for private residents of the town to come to an agreement among themselves.

Setting aside for the moment the somewhat dicey issue of who exactly is "an important person," this ruling has a number of important ramifications for our discussion.[5] First, when there is no "important person," workers can make binding agreements among themselves which are then enforceable (This assumes great importance in twentieth-century Jewish discussions of labor organizing.) Second, the "important person" caveat reinforces the idea that a labor contract is not merely a private contract, but that the polis is a party to the contract.

This situation, while demonstrating that the polis has a legitimate interest in labor agreements, is still not the situation that first comes to mind when we think of labor contracts. The baseline labor contracts are between an employer and a worker and not among workers in a guild or a union. On the other hand, as we will see, this is the conceptual opening that developed into an affirmation of labor unions and organizing in the twentieth century.

The Shift to Modernity

One of the transformations of the discourse around labor in modernity is the recognition that workers and employers are not operating on a level playing field. Employers have far more power than workers, and therefore, the courts and legal institutions have a duty to protect workers. This constitutes a radical shift from the understanding that a labor agreement was contracted between equals. In the wake of this conceptual shift came a number of legal innovations including wage and hour laws, child labor laws, and collective bargaining. Another major advance was the legalization of trade unions. Trade unions leveled the playing field by giving workers the power to stop production and profits—a power equivalent to an owner's power to fire and stop paying salaries.[6]

The labor movement which engendered this conceptual shift, together with the strong ties between socialist ideals and Zionism, forced many halachic thinkers and adjudicators to revisit the issue of the labor relationship within the context of the rabbinic conceptual world that we outlined above.[7] For some, the translation of rabbinic values was pretty straightforward.

Rabbi Ben-Zion Meir Chai Uzziel (1880–1953), the *Rishon le-Tziyon* (Sephardic Chief Rabbi of the Land of Israel) responded in 1938 to several questions about the proper relationship between workers and employers. These questions were asked by the executive committee of the union of the *Hapoel Hamizrahi*, the religious workers organization. Question number 6 is titled: "The Workers' Organization and Declaring a Strike."[8]

Rabbi Uzziel begins by citing the text from the Babylonian Talmud (Baba Bathra 9a) about the two tanners, which we discussed above.[9] He comments on the story by citing the late thirteenth and early fourteenth century Spanish Sage Rabbenu Asher.

> Rabbenu Asher derived from here that all craftsmen can contract between themselves and they are considered the "residents of the town" in regard to work, and an "important

123

person" is someone like Rava who was a leader in the city—
even all the residents of the town have no right to contract
except with the agreement of the important person.

He comments on Rabbenu Asher's interpretation that: "This
is decided law upon which there is no debate," and he draws the
following conclusion which is obvious to him:

> Behold it is explicit that the sages OBM recognized the
> regulations of a craftsman's guild or union of laborers or
> clerks in the general labor federation, or other federations of
> professionals.

Rabbi Uzziel's conclusion is that a union or other professional
guild is recognized in the same way as the *bnei ha'ir*, the residents
of the city, in that they can make enforceable regulations
and ordinances. Rabbi Uzziel goes the next step with the following:

> Reason also dictates that we should not leave the worker
> alone, isolated as an individual, so that he would have to hire
> himself out for minimal wages in order to satisfy his and his
> family's hunger with bread and water in meager quantities
> and with a dark and dank apartment. In order to protect
> himself the law gave him the legal right to organize, and to
> create regulations for his fellows for the fair and equitable
> division of labor amongst them and the attaining of dignified
> treatment and appropriate payment for his work—so that he
> might support his family at the same standard of living as
> other residents of his city.

He further states that the "standard of living" includes access
to cultural institutions to advance a worker's knowledge of art and
science, and institutions in which workers can learn Torah, hospitals
and convalescent homes, and even a retirement pension. "For with
every passing day the worker's strength is dissipated, and he cannot
continue in his labors at the same pace as in his youth."

Rabbi Uzziel here makes two important sets of juridical
moves. First, he moves smoothly from the individual workers who

contract amongst themselves (i.e., the tanners) to guilds, professional organizations, and unions. This interpretation is grounded in the statement that we saw above that the residents of the city can make and enforce regulations concerning work rules. He then reads this with Rabbenu Asher's understanding that the members of a specific guild or profession are the total of the "residents of the city" as far as regulating that guild or profession is concerned. Finally, Rabbi Uzziel makes the move which crosses into modernity; he expands the scope of enforceable regulations to include those that are directed toward employers concerning living standards and not only salary.

This last move is dependent on another one. One of the assumptions that seem to be operating here is that while workers are a recognizable class—and therefore, they are "the residents of the city" for their profession—they are also in another way indistinguishable from other residents. I want to suggest that this is a strong reading of the concept of *bnei ha'ir*/residents of the city. Workers, as residents of the city, have needs that go beyond strict compensation for hours worked. In the interaction between the worker and the employer, the employer sees in the face of the worker the humanity which needs to be supported not only through minimal wages but through the ability to live a robust cultural existence, that is, to be able to be a full person.

Rabbi Uzziel's thinking is echoed (though not repeated exactly) in the decisions of a number of other important scholars. In 1945, Rabbi Eliezer Waldenberg (again in a letter to the *Hapoel Hamizrachi*) recognized the right of workers to organize and to have their regulations and rules seen as binding. He also recognized, in certain conditions, their right to strike. Rabbi Moshe Feinstein in a number of Responsa concurred. Rabbi Feinstein's concise answer (in a 1951 Responsa) to the question of whether unions were permitted in Jewish law was, "I do not see any possibility of their being forbidden. The opposite is the case . . ."[10] Feinstein expanded the scope of the *bnei ha'ir* category to include permitting striking workers to prevent scabs from doing their jobs—since the union is considered the *bnei ha'ir*, their ordinances (such as calling a strike) must be heeded.[11]

Chapter 6: Labor

The Important Person / Adam Hashuv

A unique and important aspect of the Talmud's discussion
of workers in the text that we cited above (BT Baba Bathra 9a) is
the presence of "an important person." The binding nature of
agreements reached between residents acting as "the residents of
the town" is limited to situations in which there is no "important
person." However, "where there is an 'important person,' not
everyone . . . can reach a binding agreement." The agreement
must be reached with the approval of the important person, or the
important person could abrogate the agreement.

What constitutes an important person?

Joseph ibn Migash (1077–1141), a Spanish scholar, articulated
the broad consensus up to his time in the following manner: "[One
who] is a learned scholar and appointed to leadership of the
community." In other words, to qualify as "an important person,"
one must meet two criteria—erudition and appointed leadership.
Maimonides in the thirteenth century adds something new to the
definition. He describes an *adam hashuv* as "an important sage
[who can] correct the actions of the place and cause the ways of its
inhabitants to succeed." This fits with his definition of one who has
reached the height of the religio-philosophical path at the end of his
Guide of the Perplexed.

> [T]he perfection of man that may truly be gloried in is
> the one acquired by him who has achieved, in a measure
> corresponding to his capacity, apprehension of Him, may He
> be exalted, and who knows His providence extending over
> His creatures as manifested in the act of bringing them into
> being and in their governance as it is. (III:54) [12]

This is defined as "there should come from you loving-
kindness, righteousness and judgment in the earth . . ." In other
words, the perfected person, like the *adam hashuv*, is one who
understands that God's providence is perceived in bringing loving-
kindness, righteousness, and judgment on earth. The "important
person" for Maimonides is a version of a philosopher king for a city.
The *adam hashuv* is the person that ensures righteousness.

This leads to a certain degree of difficulty in figuring out who would be considered an important person in a contemporary situation. Moshe Feinstein abandons the search and declares that there is no important person now (i.e., in his time). Therefore, the decisions of the unions (the *bnei ha'ir*) are final.

Rabbi Uzziel comes to a different conclusion. He recognizes that the state of the workplace in contemporary times is beyond the ability of any single "important person"—as learned and objective as they could be—to fully grasp and be able to adjudicate. He proposes the creation of a robust labor law and a special labor court based on that law. The laws would be written by "scholars of Torah law and men of science who understand economics and market conditions." All subsequent labor disputes would be adjudicated by a standing court comprised of judges who would rule according to these laws.[13]

The important person is then assimilated into an institution which is meant to represent the righteousness of the community. This panel is Maimonides's "important sage [who can] correct the actions of the place and cause the ways of its inhabitants to succeed," as seen through a more humble lens.

Economic Justice and the Community of Obligation

As we said at the beginning of this chapter, the relationship between workers and management is complicated and therefore extremely fraught. Since the relationship is based on economic interests, it seems to be taken out of the scope of other relationships, which are based on a face-to-face encounter between two individuals. However, the rabbinic notion of the *bnei ha'ir* constantly brings us back to the recognition that although workers and management might have different economic interests which are at times conflicting, they have similar obligations within the parameters of the city. Economic justice, at heart, is based on the recognition that a worker is a person who, in order to be a fully actualized human being, needs more than just money. The relationship (even the monetary relationship) between workers and owners is grounded in this recognition that in order to create a just society, the humanity of workers must be recognized. This humanity can be actualized only with access to health care, education, cultural opportunities, housing, etc. This, of course, cannot be only the responsibility of an individual employer. At the same time, each employer must see her workers as different from their machines, as persons whose needs must be responded to.

This, it seems to me, is the deeper understanding of Rav's response to Rabbah bar bar Hana's question, "Is this the law?" "Yes," said Rav. "Because it says: 'So follow the way of the good, and keep to the paths of the just'"(Prov. 2:20).

Walking the Talk

In a community of obligation, the relationship between worker and employer does not exist in isolation. As a resident of the city, it is incumbent upon me to do what I can in order to ensure that relationships between workers and employers are just, and recognize when they are unjust. This often means taking the side of workers in labor disputes, standing with workers so that they are not made invisible by the power of large corporations. This can take many forms.

One of the current labor struggles across the United States has as its goal achieving a living wage for all workers. The federal minimum wage (which is currently $7.25/hr.), since its enactment in 1938 (at $0.25/hr.), has never been enough to raise a family of four above the poverty line.[14] In real dollars, the minimum wage has been in decline since 1968 (when it was $9.47/hr. in 2007 dollars). The federal minimum wage, which is standard across the country, does not take into account the different economic or social circumstances of workers. It is the perfect example of treating a worker as her work. State minimum wages also don't take into account the varying economic realities of living in different parts of a state or the economic situation of a specific family.

A living wage, on the other hand, is a dynamic calculation which is based on typical monthly expenses in specific geographic locations.[15] For this reason, the living wage in Los Angeles County, California, according to this calculus ($11.99) would be very different from the living wage in Bourbon County, Kansas ($6.65).[16] Living wages begin to recognize that workers are people who are not merely their labor, but who also need housing and education and so on. A simple living wage is not a panacea. The worker living in Los Angeles making $11.99 an hour would do fine if he had no dependents. If, however, he was the sole supporter of a family of four, he would have to be making $34.07.[17]

Some businesses are already recognizing that living wages are good for them (well-trained, steady work force) and also, perhaps, that this is an issue that they will ultimately lose.[18] However, many businesses are resisting. It is important—as a first step toward transforming our cities into just cities and communities of obligation—that we support living wage ordinances in our cities. However, there is a far greater scandal. Wage theft has reached such proportions in Los Angeles (and New York and Chicago) that there is a need to pass laws against wage theft. To restate this, there is a need to pass a law that defines penalties for people who don't pay their workers the money they contracted to pay them. This is not an insignificant problem either. According to a study by the Institute for Research on Labor and Employment, "low-wage workers in Los Angeles regularly experience violations of basic laws that mandate a minimum wage and overtime pay and are frequently forced to work off the clock or during their breaks. . . . Almost 30 percent of the LA workers sampled were paid less than the minimum wage in the work week preceding the survey. . . ."[19]

In industries where workers are organized and represented by unions, labor negotiations are often open to the public and having community representatives there, both clergy and laity, reminds the negotiators that the community has a stake in the just outcome of the negotiations.

When management in the hotel industry or real estate developers refuse to meet with labor, it is important for members of the community to demand meetings with management to remind them that they are operating a business in a community which cares about economic justice.[20] When a car wash locks out its workers days before Christmas as a weapon against the organizing efforts of those workers, we must stand with the workers and help them sustain themselves and their families.[21] In extreme situations when management takes actions that are unilateral and unjust, such as the Hyatt Hotel's firing of senior workers in order to replace them with nonunion entry-level workers, we might be called upon to go to the streets in demonstrations and boycotts.[22] We must unequivocally state that the workers are people whose lives are important to the community.

In all these situations, the goal is not merely organizing for power, but creating a just polis. We are the *bnei ha'ir*/the residents of the city and in that capacity we are morally empowered and obligated to intervene in labor situations in order to prevent injustice. There is no completely private contracting.

We must also remember to turn this gaze upon ourselves. Domestic workers, those who clean our houses and care for our children must also be treated justly and fairly. We must see those intimate strangers, who allow us to fulfill our potential and lead our lives, as others to whose needs we must also respond.[23] It is only as we see labor as a relationship and not as a commodity that we move closer to having justice in the city.

Notes

[1] Statement attributed to Rabbi Eliezer, *Avot deRabbi Nathan*, 2:21 (ed. Shechter, p. 44); Cf. "Shmayah said: Love work. . . ." Mishnah Avot 1:10.

[2] For example, Babylonian Talmud Nedarim 49b.

[3] See Me'ir Ayali, *Po'alim ve-omanim : melakhtam u-ma'amadam be-sifrut HaZa"L* (Yad la-Talmud, 1987)..

[4] Baba Metzia 6:1, 10d.

[5] On the question of who is an important person, see above, 126.

[6] The choice of passive verbs is not to imply that these things happened without a great deal of struggle sometimes resulting in injury and even death. I am also not claiming that modernity was the cause of the rethinking of the place and power of workers. I am saying that the mid- to late nineteenth century was when this shift occurred.

[7] See Benjamin Brown, "The Hafetz Hayim on Delayed Wages: Towards a Modernization of Halakhic Labor Law," *Tarbiz* 74:3–4 (2006): 501–538 (Hebrew).

[8]   Rabbi Ben-Zion Meir Chai Uzziel *Mishpetei Uziel* vol. 4—*Hoshen Mishpat* 42. (Accessed from the Bar Ilan Respona Project database.) The responsum is dated 4 Tevet 5698 (1938). The translation is mine.

[9]   Page 121 above.

[10]   *Igrot Moshe: Hoshen Mishpat I:58.*

[11]   Feinstein's decision on scab workers was based on union workers being a majority of the workers. In today's workplace, this is, of course, not the situation.

[12]   *Guide of the Perplexed* (vol. 2), trans. Shlomo Pines (Chicago: University of Chicago Press, 1963), 637–638.

[13]   "In practice however, I say that the contemporary workplace does not make it possible for 'an important person,' by himself, to adjudicate the legitimacy of workers' claims. Rather, in my opinion, there is a need to establish an important court consisting of scholars of Torah law and men of science who understand economics and market conditions, and they together will decide the details of labor law in all its details. Following this, judges will be appointed who will adjudicate based on this legislation in all disputes between workers relating to equitable division of labor and also between workers and management in regards to their mutual relationship." *Mishpat Uzziel* (ibid.).

[14]   http://oregonstate.edu/instruct/anth484/minwage.html
(accessed on August 21, 2009). Information is based on statistics from the U.S. Bureau of the Census; U.S. Department of Labor, Bureau of Labor Statistics; Statistical Abstract of the United States; and Survey of Current Business.

[15]   Food, child care, medical, housing, transportation.

[16]   Figures are from the *Living Wage Calculator,*
http://www.livingwage.geog.psu.edu/ (accessed August 21, 2009).

[17] $23.26 in Bourbon County.

[18]   Peter Dumon, "A 'Living Wage' Is Money in the Bank," *Los Angeles Times* (June 11, 2008).

[19]   Ana Luz Gonzalez Ruth Milkman, Victor Narro, *Wage Theft and Workplace Violations in Los Angeles: The Failure of Employment and Labor Law for Low-Wage Workers* (UCLA Institute for Research on Labor and Employment, 2010), 1–2.

[20]   Security guards are ultimately dependent on real estate developers for their salaries. Even though the security guards are hired by subcontractors, if a developer refuses to agree to a raise in salary or benefits, the subcontractor is powerless to proceed on their own. "Two years ago, four thousand security officers in Los Angeles's commercial-office buildings negotiated with leading building owners and responsible security contractors, creating a historic agreement that brought them health care, decent wages, and sick days." R. M. Arietta, "'Reel Profits, Real Poverty': Security Guards Organize in Hollywood," *In These Times,* February 4, 2010.

[21] Samantha Page, "Former Employees Protest Marina Car Wash's Abrupt Firings," *Venice Patch* (December 15, 2010).

[22] Katie Johnston Chase, "A Hard Ending for Housekeepers," *Boston Globe* (2009). Cf. Ryan Torok, "Rabbi, AJU Professor Arrested at Hotel Workers Protest," *Jewish Journal* (July 23, 2010).

[23] New York State passed the nation's first Domestic Workers Rights Bill in July 2010. Nichols Confessore, "Domestic Workers' Rights Bill Passes," in *City Room* (New York City: The New York Times Company, 2010). "Domestic workers (along with agricultural workers) were one of the few categories of workers excluded from the Fair Labor Standards Act (FLSA) and the National Labor Relations Act in the 1930s because of opposition by white southern congressmen who insisted on control over the largely black southern workforce. After 1974, domestic workers were included in FLSA minimum wage laws, but baby sitters and companions for the elderly are still not guaranteed minimum wage, and live-in workers are not assured overtime pay. Moreover, domestic workers don't have the right to organize and bargain collectively and are excluded from the Occupational Safety and Health Act and civil rights employment laws, which only apply to workplaces with 15 or more employees." Premilla Nadasen, "Domestic Worker Bill of Rights Passes New York Senate," in *Ms.blog* (Ms. Magazine, 2010).

Chapter 7

Restorative Justice

This is what justice can look like.

Veronica (not her real name) is a seventeen-year-old from a solid working-class Mexican American family. She has never been in trouble with the law. The very idea that she would be in trouble with the law is foreign to her parents. In her senior year in high school, Veronica finds out that she is failing a class that she needs to graduate. When she gets the notice, Veronica fears that her life is ruined. If she doesn't graduate, she will not be able to go to college. If she doesn't go to college, she won't be able to get a job and so on. She hides the notice in her room and doesn't tell her parents.

The next morning on her way to school, Veronica passes one of the department stores in the neighborhood. She wanders into the store and then she walks from department to department aimlessly. As she moves through the store, she begins putting items in her shoulder bag: a music CD, a bottle of inexpensive perfume, tissues, a T-shirt. It is not clear if there was a specific moment when she formulated the intention to steal these items, and yet there she was leaving the store without paying. As she leaves the store, she is stopped by security. Her bag is opened, the stolen items are found, she is arrested, and her parents are called to take her home.

I am now, months later, sitting with Veronica, her parents and the loss-prevention officer for the department store chain in an upstairs office at the store. Under California law, certain juvenile offenses can be resolved under "diversion programs." I am a mediator for one such program—the Jewish Community Justice Program.

Over the next two hours, I facilitate a conversation between Veronica and Frank (not his real name), the loss-prevention officer. Veronica tells her story first, starting with failing her course and ending with her parents picking her up. I prompt her with, "And then what happened?" and "And how did that feel?" When she describes her arrest and her mother having to take off from work to retrieve her at the police station, her embarrassment and regret are palpable and her tears flow.

When she is done, Frank tells his story. He talks about the responsibility of being a loss-prevention officer. He tells of the hardship that a wave of shoplifting could potentially cause to a community if a store is convinced that it is losing too much money. He talks about the potential of lost jobs and lost opportunities.

When Frank finishes, I ask Veronica if she wants to make the situation right and what she is prepared to do to facilitate that. Veronica suggests that she could perhaps do some community service, perhaps write a letter of apology. I ask Frank if this sounds appropriate or if he has something else in mind. Frank says that he wants three things. He wants a letter from Veronica telling him that she has enrolled in a Graduate Equivalency Degree (GED) course. He wants another letter telling him that she has reached the half-way mark in the course, and finally he wants a letter from Veronica when she completes her GED.

The room is silent. Finally, Veronica—crying—agrees and says thank you. I draw up a contract which Veronica, her parents, and Frank sign. Veronica walked into the room thinking her life was over and walks out feeling that she is a member of a community that actually cares about her and is interested in enabling her to further her ambitions. In turn, I am sure, she walks away with a feeling of love for and commitment to the community.

That is what justice could look like.

Atonement and Justice

Mishnah Yoma says the following about Yom Hakipurim, the Day of Atonement:

> Transgressions that are between a person and God, the Day of Atonement atones[1] for. Transgressions that are between a person and his fellow, the Day of Atonement does not atone for, until that person appeases his fellow.

This Mishnaic statement, especially the second half of this statement, has been the grist for many sermonic mills from the time it was inscribed in the Jewish textual memory. What are the implications of the claim that Yom Hakipurim does not affect forgiveness for sins between people until there is reconciliation between the parties? What is "reconciliation?"

To answer the second question first, the Palestinian Talmud attributes the following to the Babylonian sage of the late second and early third century, Samuel.[2]

> The one who has transgressed against his fellow, must say to him: 'I have sinned against you.' If he accepts [the apology], it is well. If not, he brings people and apologizes in front of them. This is what is written: "He looks upon[3] [*yashor*] men," he should make a row [*shurah*] of men. "And he says: 'I have sinned; I have perverted what was right; But I was not paid back for it.'" About him Scripture states: "He redeemed him from passing into the Pit; He will enjoy the light."[4]

A similar procedure is outlined in the Babylonian Talmud[5] and is subsequently codified as law.[6] a direct interaction between the offender and the one against whom the offender has transgressed is prescribed. In that interaction, the offender must state clearly that he has sinned. If his apology is not accepted, he must raise the stakes and apologize before a group of people.[7] If this procedure is not followed, the person does not obtain atonement.

Is the implication here that the reason a person should ask forgiveness for transgressions from the injured party, is only to obtain atonement from God? What is the connection, if any, between atonement, forgiveness, and the legal system or the judiciary?

In this chapter, I will argue that asking forgiveness is not incidental to the legal process of redress, nor does it take its place. Asking forgiveness in a face-to-face encounter is the end goal of the judicial process, whose purpose is to restore or repair the community.[8] This claim about repairing the community itself stands on two other claims: The first is that human character is corrigible and not immutable. The mutability of human character is based on a belief in free will. The second claim is that justice is dependent on recognizing the dignity of everyone in the community.

Restorative vs. Punitive Justice

There are two different notions of systemic justice.[9] One is restorative or reparative, and the other is punitive. The goal of a punitive justice system is to inflict punishment on the wrongdoer. The goal of the punishment is either deterrence—in which scenario the potential transgressors will be made aware that there is a price to pay for their transgression and that, therefore, "crime does not pay."[10] The other possible goal of the punishment is vengeance in which the society is given the opportunity to avenge itself upon the wrongdoer and in that doing restore its lost honor or erase its shame.[11]

The goal of restorative justice is to restore the community to its state prior to the disruption or tear that resulted from the transgression.[12] The model for restorative justice is that the offender and the victim meet face-to-face (or sometimes, at the discretion of the victim through a mediator) so that the offender realizes the real harm caused to a real person, and the person transgressed against realizes that the offender is also a human being.[13]

The irony of the punitive approach is that while it claims to be operating on behalf of the victim, the truth is that the victim is almost totally left out of the equation. The state pursues a prosecution against the offender. However, in the restorative paradigm, the victim is involved at every stage.

If, as I have argued in the first part of this book, the model of a city that emerges from the rabbinic textual tradition is that of a community of obligation, we would expect the texts to support a restorative justice model. At the heart of a community of obligation is the web of relationships that engenders obligations between residents who are otherwise anonymous to each other. The tearing of this web can lead to serious repercussions in the vitality of the community.[14] It would thus be appropriate for the textual tradition that nurtures this model to also further a restorative and reparative justice system. This, in fact, is what we find.

Forgiveness and Justice

Mishnah Baba Kama 8:7

Even though [the offender] gives [the victim] [monetary compensation for the damage, medical expenses, time lost from working, pain and suffering and humiliation], he is not forgiven until he asks for forgiveness from the victim.

For it says: "Therefore, restore the man's wife—since he is a prophet, he will intercede for you—to save your life" (Gen. 20:7).

From where do we know that the forgiver should not be cruel?

For it says: "Abraham then prayed to God, and God healed Abimelech . . ." (Gen. 20:17)

This Mishnah describes an interaction which includes a number of steps. First, there was an offense. The specific context of this Mishnah in Baba Kama is physical injury, but it is not necessarily limited to physical injury.[15] There is a judgment rendered against the tortfeasor which must be paid. This, however, is not the end of the process. The tortfeasor must then approach the victim and ask for forgiveness. It is only at this stage of the process that the wrong can be righted—and it is only in a face-to-face interaction. At the same time, "the forgiver should not be cruel." When approached, the injured party should (in a reasonable period of time) forgive the offender.[16]

There is an ideology, and possibly even a theology, which undergirds this legal approach. People choose to act in certain ways. They can act well or poorly, yet they are not defined by their actions. a person is not incorrigibly evil. A person has done something bad. This bad action can be atoned for and the victim of the action can, and should, help in this process of atoning, at the end of which the offender is no longer an "offender," the victim is no longer a "victim," and the community has been restored. This understanding of human action is at the very heart of any concept of repentance and free will in the Jewish textual tradition.

This understanding of the mutability of human character is articulated in a story in Babylonian Talmud Berachot 10a.

The Sage, Her Husband, and the Ruffians

The story is part of a longer text which begins by discussing how differentiation might be quantified in the context of the earliest time for the recitation of the *sh'ma* prayer.[17] The heroes of the story are the Palestinian sage R. Meir and his wife Bruria, with a strong supporting role played by a group of ruffians. In its own way, the story touches upon issues of essentialism and nonessentialism, polysemy and midrash, the gendered boundaries of interpretation.

The first line of the *story* might well be seen as its title:

> There were these rebels/ruffians/thugs [*biryony*] who were in Rabbi Meir's neighborhood.

The scene is set, the protagonists are named, the dramatic conflict is imminent. The great sage R. Meir has the misfortune of gaining a band of ruffians for neighbors. Who were these *biryony*? The only *biryony* of whom we have some knowledge are the group who, in the collection of Aggadot about the destruction of the Temple in Bavli Gittin (56a), forced the Jews under siege in Jerusalem to fight by not allowing anyone to leave and by burning the grain stores. One of the *biryony* is identified as Abba Sikra, a name that is tantalizingly close to the Greek term *sikarios* or assassins. There is some ambiguity as to the etymology of the word *biryony*. Urbach has suggested that it might be a negatively tinged diminutive of *briyah*, creature.[18] Sokoloff defines it as "outlaw," related to the Akkadian *baranu*, rebel.[19]

One is tempted to apply a hermeneutics of suspicion to the Talmudic naming of the *biryony* and see them as a group not under the sway of the rabbis. Or, perhaps, they were just ruffians.

It is also unclear from this first line what the relationship between R. Meir and the ruffians is. Is there merely a geographic proximity? Are they engaged in some manner of social intercourse? The next line in the story seems to supply an answer:

> They would annoy [*metza'aru*] him greatly.

The verb that the *aggadist* chose here "annoy" "*metza'aru*" is interesting. It is ambiguous to the point of incomprehension. Did the mere presence of the ruffians annoy R. Meir? Were they chucking (Late Antique) beer bottles at him as he was on his way to the study hall? Usages in the Bavli of the verb *metza'ar* when it is an action that one does to another, run a rather large gamut: "annoy," "torture," "make physically uncomfortable."[20] It is also used to mark either an intergroup polemical attack (as with a Sadducee) or an intragroup polemical attack (as with R. Yehoshua and R. Eliezer). Further, whose voice is represented in this line? Is it the omniscient narrator who is then giving the imprimatur of truth to R. Meir's feelings: "They really were annoying him. They were bad." Or, perhaps, is this a representation of R. Meir's opinion through a fallible narrator, thereby reinforcing the subjective nature of *metza'aru*, annoying. Are we observing a scene from a neutral vantage point, or are we inside R. Meir's head?

The next line is R. Meir's response to his situation:

Rabbi Meir prayed for them, that they should die.

This line is striking. As we read the line we think, "Oh, R. Meir is going to pray for them. That's good." Then we are hit with the purpose of R. Meir's prayer: "that they should die." The reader's expectations are reinforced by the literal translation of the phrase here rendered as "prayed for them" —*ka ba'iy rahmy*/he requested mercy or love—and then completely frustrated. Additionally, R. Meir presents a very straightforward theology of prayer: one prays and God fulfills the prayer.[21]

At this point the second protagonist enters.

Bruria, his wife, said to him: "What are you thinking?"

This intervention on the part of Bruria should be read with the force of the colloquial English "What were you thinking?" Apparently Bruria found out, heard or intuited that R. Meir was praying for the demise of the ruffians and was, at the least, disturbed. R. Meir, not to be swayed, answers:

"For it is written: Let sinners (*hata'im*) cease [out of the earth, and let the wicked be no more.]" (Ps. 104:35)

To paraphrase R. Meir—and I do think that the story works better literarily if we assign this line to R. Meir even though it can be understood as either R. Meir or Bruria—"I am merely following the explicit precedent of King David who articulated this very prayer: 'Let sinners cease. . . .' What else might that mean aside from let them die?!"

Bruria responds sharply:

> "Is it written: 'Sinners (*hot'im*)'? Rather, 'sins (*hata'im*)' is written.
> And further, continue to the end of the verse 'and the wicked be no more.'
> Since sins will cease the evil will be evil no more.

Bruria challenges R. Meir's reading of the verse. This is not, however, a challenge to R. Meir's ability to decode biblical Hebrew. R. Meir is, of course, right that contextually *hata'im* means sinners. Bruria's challenge is of a different nature. She is challenging R. Meir's method of reading or method of interpretation. R. Meir is reading the verse in a literalist fashion. That is, on a strict philological analysis the word as spelled, pointed, and contextualized "means" sinners. Bruria's claim is for polysemy, for a wider semantic spectrum, for a different reading methodology, ultimately for midrash.

To channel Bruria for a moment, she would make the following claim: the right way to read a verse, or understand a word in a verse is not merely through its local context, but rather to see its full semantic field as contextualized in the largest context of what we might call Judaism. While in biblical Hebrew *hata'im* means sinners, in Rabbinic Hebrew *hata'im* as a rule is used to mean sins. This part of the semantic field is then open to us as midrashic readers. The resulting reading of *sins* will cease is reinforced by the latter part of the verse. As is well known, one of the axioms of midrash is that there are no redundancies in the Torah. If the second half of the verse in Psalms was merely meant as a poetic repetition, what use might it have?[22] It should therefore be read, "*Sins* will cease from the land, and the wicked will be not [wicked] anymore." Since there will be no sins, there will be no sinners.

Bruria is making a claim about midrash at the same time that she is making a claim about human nature. Analogously to midrash, people are not static. Sometimes they do good things and sometimes bad. If a person sins, that person is not then necessarily a "sinner," rather a person who has sinned. To paraphrase another late antique tradition from Christianity: hate the sin and love the sinner.[23]

Bruria continues with a statement that is also, ultimately, a competing claim about prayer:

> "Rather, pray for them to return in repentance, and [they will be] evil no more."

Bruria redirects R. Meir's prayer. R. Meir should pray for these *biryony* to repent. If they repent, they will no longer be wicked since they will no longer be sinning. What might it mean for R. Meir to pray for these folks to repent? Repentance is a result of choice and intent. Can R. Meir pray that his annoying neighbors repent, and as a result of his prayer they repent in the same way as a prayer, for rain brings rain or a prayer for a little red wagon brings a little red wagon? Even within a simplistically causal theology in which prayers are answered by divine fiat, repentance doesn't quite fit. To repent, one must exercise will, make choices, exhibit intent. How can one "repent" as a result of divine intercession? How can one be said to have chosen freely to have repented if that was a result of an intercession which short-circuited that very expression of free choice? Bruria was actually telling R. Meir that he should just pray for them. This prayer was a prayer for R. Meir. This prayer was the concretization of R. Meir's realization that his neighbors were not essentially evil. The continuation and ending of the *story* play out this narrative arc.

> He prayed for them.
> They returned in repentance.

There are two actions here that occur serially. R. Meir prays, and they repent. One might say that it was R. Meir letting go of the essentialist definition of his neighbors as *biryony* and sinners who should be killed that allowed them to see themselves as able to repent and change. Ultimately, though, it is R. Meir who has changed. Bruria has introduced him to a midrashic understanding of text, prayer, and the world. She has also introduced him to a way of reading: Texts are polysemic, not static. Prayer is, in large part, for oneself. People are not essentially but only contingently defined by their actions.

This is at the heart of the restorative justice claim. People are responsible for their actions but are not defined by their actions. The interaction between a person who transgressed and the person who suffered the injury is a healing one.[24] The transgressor is afforded the opportunity to realize both the hurt that was caused by their action and also that they are not eternally defined by that transgression. The injured party can come to understand that the offender is a full human being beyond the offense and in that realization enable the offender to re-enter the community. Therefore, people must make restitution for their misdeeds, and then they must have a way to repair the fabric of the community, and the community must reintegrate them.[25]

The other principle on which the ideology of reparative restorative justice rests is the recognition of the "victim" as an Other—that is, a person with full humanity. This is discussed in one of the more famous discussions in Talmudic literature, that concerning the biblical law of "eye for an eye."

Lex Talionis

"An eye for an eye makes the whole world blind." This sentiment, attributed to Mahatma Gandhi and Martin Luther King, Jr., neatly sums up contemporary rhetoric about the principle known as *lex talionis*, or the law of the talion, defined in the OED as "the principle of exacting compensation, 'eye for eye, tooth for tooth.'"[26] The law, whose origin is in Exodus 21:23–26,[27] is commonly understood as an extreme response to violence. The Torah writes,

> But if other damage ensues, the penalty shall be life for life,
> eye for eye, tooth for tooth, hand for hand, foot for foot,
> burn for burn, wound for wound, bruise for bruise.

Popular opinion has it that this form of justice was done away with by the rabbis of the Mishnah and the Talmud, who all agreed that the biblical injunction is not to be taken literally but rather implies monetary compensation. The traditional opinion is well represented in this quote from Maimonides's code of Jewish Law, the *Mishneh Torah*:

> For if one cut off the hand or leg of his fellow, we evaluate [the victim] as if he was a slave sold in the market—[estimating] how much he was worth [before] and how much he is worth now—and [the offender] pays the depreciation, for it says "eye for [*tahat*] eye." They learned from the tradition that the word *tahat* refers to monetary payment.[28]

It is only in the case of "life for life" that the talion is retained.

The contemporary scholarly *vox populi* is well represented by David Novak's theoretical formulation of the justification for superseding the talion.

> Monetary compensation is the best we can do under these imperfect circumstances. Money is the *tertium quid* [third thing AC] that introduces a standard whereby a just commensurate relation can be stipulated between the assailant and the assaulted.
> To attempt to practice literal equality by physical means in cases of physical injury would result in real inequality in the end. As the examples brought in the Babylonian Talmud indicate, that would result in a legal assault on the human dignity of the assailant as serious as the original assault on his or her victim.[29]

We will examine the examples brought by the Babylonian Talmud below to see if they actually accord with this understanding of them. For now, we note that the opposition to talion is that monetary compensation brings about a more "commensurate relation" which is therefore more "just." Novak elsewhere states this as "money can be equalized in a way that body parts cannot be."[30] We must ask, "Is this true?" That is, is monetary compensation equal to the injury in a way that the offender's body part is not?

I want to raise the possibility, following William Ian Miller,[31] that this is not the case. Miller claims that the talion should be understood not as a liability claim (as it is in the popular imagination) or as punitive retribution, but as a property claim. This is to say that when I knock out your eye, by that act you own my eye. This is the starting point for negotiations. What would I pay to buy your eye— that is, to retain it in my head. In this situation you, the victim of my aggression, are in a much stronger position. If we were merely haggling over the loss of your sight and its impact on your life and so on, I, the offender, would be in the stronger position, arguing that there was not that much damage and you were not that handy with your eyes anyway (you were, for example, color-blind or astigmatic or didn't like reading). However, if I am faced with the prospect of surrendering my eye (which now belongs to you), I would not be so niggardly. I would be much more forthcoming if the actual choice were to be either payment or losing my own eye.[32] In this sense, one could argue that the talion brings about a far more just outcome than the abstraction of equivalent compensation.[33] The purpose of the talion, understood in this way, is "getting to even" rather than our notion of "getting even."[34]

While I just said that the talion is more just and puts the victim in a stronger position, I am not claiming that this will necessarily bring us to a "correct" dollar amount for the assault. The insight that moves the talion, at least rabbinically, is that an assault upon the body is an assault upon the humanity of a person. This assault is rectified when a person's humanity is restored. For this reason, ultimately, Jewish law, halacha, does not follow the opinion that claims that "eye for eye" means just that. Jewish law substitutes compensation. However, we will see that the law is troubled by the fact that monetary compensation, based upon a liability structure (i.e., what is the depreciation in the victim's worth as an object of market value) falls into the trap of re-assaulting the victim.

The rest of this chapter will unfold by way of trying to retain this insight, while minimizing the possibility of actual bloodshed, allowing us to articulate a more powerful notion of restorative justice. The way forward is, of course, through the Bavli.

The Sugya[35]

The question of whether the talion is understood as literal is discussed and seemingly decided in the Tannaitic midrashim recorded in the fifth and sixth century but seemingly pointing to an earlier time (second and third century CE) when the sages cited in the midrashim lived. Further, the Mishnah which generates this very sugya[36] does not even mention the possibility of the talion. The Mishnah only speaks the language of monetary compensation.[37] Finally, the first sugya on this Mishnah reaches the conclusion that an eye for eye must mean money.[38] It is surprising to the reader then, that the discussion is reopened in the next sugya, the text we are going to analyze now.[39] I will briefly review the structure of the entire sugya and then analyze parts of it in greater depth as necessary.

The sugya is comprised of four Tannaitic texts and four Amoraic texts, all making the same basic claim—that the biblical talion actually means monetary compensation. A discussion following each of these texts argues the opposite point—that the talion cannot mean monetary compensation which would then be unfair for one or another reason, but it must refer to the actual talion. The discussions following the first two Tannaitic texts and the first three Amoraic texts conclude with the proposition that "eye for eye" must be understood literally [*mamash*]. In other words, these discussions overturn the seemingly settled idea that "eye for eye" refers to monetary compensation. The discussion generated by the last two of the Tannaitic units and the last of the Amoraic units uphold the proposition that "eye for eye" actually refers to monetary compensation.

Here is the first unit. It follows the basic structure of all the units. a text is quoted which states (and sometimes, as in the first text, supports the statement with an argument) that "eye for eye" should be understood as monetary compensation. This statement is then challenged and either overthrown or supported. The first unit is generated by a Tannaitic text and is overthrown:

It is taught [in a baraita]:[40]
R. Dosthai b. Yehudah says: "Eye for eye" — [this is] money.
You say money, or is it, in fact, an eye?
You stated, Behold if this one's eye was larger, and this one's
eye was smaller — how can that be "eye for eye?"

> And if you were to say that in these types of situation, [the
> victim] takes money from [the offender],[41]

The Torah says: "You shall have one law" — a law that is equal
to all of you.

> I say, what is the difficulty?
> Perhaps [one should say] he took sight from him [the
> victim], the Merciful One [*Rahmana*] says we should take
> sight from him [the offender].
> For if you are not to say thus, a small person who killed
> a large person, and a large person who kills a small
> person, how can you kill him.
> Rather, he [the murderer] took a soul from him [the
> victim], the Merciful One [*Rahmana*] said take a soul from
> him [the murderer].
> Here too, he took sight from him, the Merciful One said,
> we should take sight from him [the offender].[42]

The unit opens with the baraita. R. Dosthai b. Yehudah claims
an "eye for eye" refers to monetary compensation. This principle
is challenged by the rhetorical question: perhaps it does actually
mean what it says, that is an eye for an eye. This rhetorical challenge
is fought off with the possibility that going down this road would
lead to absurdities. What if the attacker had a large eye but he put
out the victim's small eye? How, if we then put out the attacker's
eye, would this constitute "eye for eye?"[43] The stam (the anonymous
voice in the sugya) raises the possibility that in some cases where
actual and equal retribution is impossible, the court would fall back
on monetary compensation. This, however, is dismissed since it
would abrogate the principle derived midrashically from Exodus 24
that justice need be applied equally to every case. There could not,
then, be one case of physical retribution and another of monetary
compensation.

The stam then saves the possibility of physical talion by
recasting the injury. It is not a specific eye that was lost, but sight.
In that case, appropriate and equal retaliation would be to cause

the attacker's sight to be lost. The principle of "eye for eye" is then saved. An interesting aspect of this argument is that it draws on the argument which no authority contradicts, which is "life for life." For the editorial voice of this sugya, capital punishment is a given. If we are going to get all tangled up in the minute physicality of the exchange of a life for a life, we would not be able to execute a three-hundred-pound murderer for killing a one-hundred-fifty-pound victim—or vice versa.[44] This *reductio ad absurdum* argument allows the stam to recover the talion by analogy to "life for life" rather than "body for body."

And so it goes. The next unit is generated by a baraita which cites Rabbi Shimon b. Yohai as the avatar of "'eye for eye'—[this is] money." His statement is challenged in the baraita with the argument that if a blind man blinded someone, or an amputee cut off another's limb, how would the court be able to carry out the judgment of "eye for eye"? The alternative that in those specific cases monetary compensation could be paid is dismissed as, again, it would not fit the rule for equal application of the law.

Talion is rescued again by analogy with capital punishment. What of the case that a terminally ill person (who is considered legally dead[45]) were to kill another? He is already legally dead, and therefore, we are not able to fulfill the precept of "eye for eye." However, we do not therefore revert to saying that the murderer in that case should compensate the victim monetarily. Rather we rely on the understanding that where it is possible to execute the judgment of "eye for eye," we do; and where it is impossible, we do not. This need not undermine the system.

We will not review the entire sugya which consists of arguments pro and con all based on statements which support the idea of monetary compensation for physical injury. Some of the arguments result in sustaining a challenge to this statement—that is, they support the idea of physical talion. Some beat back the challenge and support monetary compensation. The final movement of the sugya[46] returns to Tannaitic material. For the first time in the sugya, it is a Tanna who claims that talion means actual physical retribution.

It is taught [in a baraita]:
R. Eliezer says: "Eye for eye" —actually [an eye].
  Can you imagine [that he thinks] an actual [eye]?!
  R. Eliezer does not hold of all these Tannaim?
Raba said: This is to say that they don't assess him as a slave.
Abbaye said to him: Rather like whom [do they assess him]?
  As a free man.
  Do free men have a price?
Rather said R. Ashi: This is to say that they do not assess according to the injured party but according to the offender.

R. Eliezer claims that "eye for eye" means equal talion. This claim is scandalous for the stam, both on its own and in light of the fact that every other Tanna holds that "eye for eye" refers to monetary compensation. Raba and Abbaye are deployed to domesticate R. Eliezer's claim. There is no intention for an eye to be removed to compensate for the eye already damaged. However, the performance of the talion is retained in R. Eliezer's statement as mediated through Abbaye and Raba. It is the *offender* who is assessed as a slave to see what damage a similar injury would cause *him*. R. Ashi's claim is that R. Eliezer retains the original intent of the verse (and the original content of the talion) by moving the focus of the compensation from victim to offender. It is the offender's arm, eye, etc., which must be assessed to arrive at the appropriate compensation.

I would like to push this further. The exchange between Raba and Abbaye is very illuminating for our concerns. Raba comments on the party line (originally inscribed in the Mishnah that generates this entire discourse) that we assess the victim as a slave to ascertain the differential between his prior value and his current value. According to Raba, R. Eliezer's position is different since he does not demand that the victim be assessed as a slave. To this, Abbaye responds, what choice do we have? A free person cannot be assessed, since a free person has no price. The essential characteristic, Abbaye claims, of a free person is that they are not chattel, while the essential characteristic of a slave is that they are chattel. The only way to assess a person—or perhaps the very act of a monetary valuation of a person—assumes that the person would be a slave in the transaction.

Abbaye's claim is not only an economic claim; it is also a moral claim, a claim based on values. Abbaye's objection to Raba admits that the operation of assessment *as a slave* is an assault on the humanity of the person assessed—since the assessment imputes slavery to a free person. R. Ashi's concluding statement accords with this insight. We have no desire to again assault the humanity of the injured party. We would only assault the offender. The structure of the talion enables us to not recreate the assault when we are supposed to be offering relief.

This insight is brought to life in the actual conclusion to this sugya—a story of a father, a son, a donkey, and a court.

The Father, the Son, the Donkey, and the Court

Here then is the story:
There was a [*hamara*] donkey driver[47] who cut off the hand of a child.
He[48] came before R. Papa b. Samuel.
He [R. Papa b. Samuel] said to them: "Go assess him according to the four categories [of damage]."[49]
Raba said to him: "We however teach that there are five [categories of damage]."
He said to them: "I was speaking [of the categories] excluding 'damage.'"
Abbaye said to him: "Behold it is a donkey [*hamor*] and a donkey is considered as a bull, and a bull only pays 'damage.'"
He said to them: "Go assess his damage."
He said to him: "Behold he must be assessed as a slave.
He said to them: "Go assess him as a slave."
The father of the child said to him: "Since [he will be assessed] as a slave, I do not want it as the matter will humiliate him.
They said to him: "Behold you are obligated to the child."
He said to them: "When he grows up, I will compensate him from my pocket."

This story has two major scenes.

In the first scene, the action is centered on the judge. The case comes before the judge. The judge is the one who is acting and who is garnering responses and corrections. He starts by quoting black letter law: "Go assess him according to the four categories of damage." He is questioned, and he clarifies that he is referring to the categories in addition to "damage" which is understood. He is once again questioned, and here it becomes obvious that he is working from a written account rather than from a living person standing before him. Abbaye corrects his teacher's perception of the case (in essence, his reading of the word *hamara*) and informs him that it is a donkey. R. Papa b. Samuel, the judge, changes course and says that the victim need only be assessed for "damage." The assessment is accomplished by finding out how much he might be worth if he was sold as a slave.

This leads to the second scene. At this moment, the father of the boy intervenes. This—assessing his son as a slave—he says, is not acceptable. The father's intervention stops the proceedings. It is now the father who is the center of the action. He is questioned, and he answers. The judge is irrelevant from here on in.

The intervention of the father forces the court to confront the child as another person. Prior to the intervention of the father, the judge was not dealing with the case in terms of actual people, but rather as another text. He even misjudged as a result of an actual misreading of the case. The father forced the case off the page and into the world. At that moment, the judge was shunted off to the side. It was the father who recognized his son as a person who brought these proceedings to a halt. At the moment that the court attempted to assess the boy—that is, to regard him as an object (a "totality")—the father intervenes and points out that this is humiliating because the boy is not an object (he is an "infinity").

This story is also a corrective to the immediately preceding discussion. The purely theoretical conversation about "eye for eye" consistently treated people as objects to be compared with one another, to be assessed, to be measured, to be retaliated against. Only in the final movement in which Raba says that free men have no price is there a recognition that one cannot actually assess another person without assaulting the person's humanity. The father in the story pushes this one step further and states that one *should not* assess another person.

I want to suggest that the reason that this sugya is so troubled is that there is unease with the very notion of objectifying, thereby totalizing, the victim of an assault through treating her as a slave. This seems to duplicate the original assault which did not respect her humanity. Retaining the structure of the talion places the focus on the offender, and compensates or balances the assault on the victim with a similar assault.

While the law is settled that an offender compensates their victim with monetary compensation, this text reinforces the unease that the rabbis have with this outcome as it does not necessarily do its work to bring the victim "back to even" or to make him whole—making the victim whole in this case is recognizing her full humanity, that she is not an object.

Restorative Justice

Rabbinic justice is thus premised on two principles. First, that the goal of the judicial process is to repair that which was damaged by the offense—the property damage and the physical suffering, but also the damage to the community in the fraying of the web of relationships which constitutes the community of obligation. Second, the way to justice is by respecting the humanity of both the offender *and* the victim. Bringing the victim and the offender into engagement with each other needs result in restoring the dignity of both. Treating the victim as an object—either by assessing him as one as in the Talmudic example, or by sidelining her in the judicial proceedings as in a contemporary state prosecution—reenacts the original offense against her humanity. A justice system which respects these two principles is a restorative system.

A punitive justice system is a system, like the one that is currently operating in the United States, in which the state prosecutes an offender with the end goal being punishment, for reasons of either deterrence or vengeance. This is a system which does not seem to be working. According to Department of Justice statistics, as of June 30, 2009, there were 1,617,478 prisoners in the

U.S. prison system. This means that "about 1 in every 198 U.S. residents was imprisoned with a sentence of more than 1 year, a rate of 504 prisoners per 100,000 U.S. residents."[50] The recidivism rate for some categories of crime are in the fifty- to sixty-percent range.[51] It is hard to argue that this is an efficient way to deter crime and, furthermore, warehousing this number of prisoners is an enormous drain on the economy.

From the point of view argued in this book, where the goal is to create a community of obligation, a society that is more righteous and more just, it is hard to argue that the way from here to there runs through the incarceration of one in every hundred and ninety-eight residents of the United States.

Restorative justice projects such as the one that Veronica benefited from are far too rare in the United States, though where they exist they are effective.[52] If we are going to move our cities on to the path toward reconnecting all residents, the path on which Veronica is not alienated from her community, we must begin with rethinking the way we "do" justice. We must keep in mind that the goal of the system should be restoration of the community, not vengeance.

Notes

[1] This is not the place to pursue either of two interesting possibilities of this line: (1) that the day itself (without repentance or other activity) might affect atonement; (2) what exactly *lehkaper*, here translated as *atonement*, means. For the former, see M Yoma 8:7, T Yoma 4:5–9 (ed. Lieberman, 251–2) and the discussions in the Palestinian Talmud Yoma 8:8–9 (45b) and the Babylonian Talmud Yoma 85b, Shevuot 13a; for the latter, see Jacob Milgrom, *Leviticus 1–16: a New Translation with Introduction and Commentary*, 1st ed., the Anchor Bible (Doubleday, 1991), 708 where he famously interprets the verb *k-p-r* as purging rather than atoning.

[2] Yoma 8:9, 45c. Cf. PT Yoma 8:7, 6c.

[3] Translating here with the King James Version to keep the midrashic sense.

[4] The verses are Job 33:26–27.

[5] Yoma 87a. In the Bavli, a statement similar to the first part of Samuel's statement is attributed to a Palestinian sage of the fourth century, R. Yitzhak, while a procedure similar to the second half of Samuel's statement is attributed to R. Hisda, a Babylonian sage of the fourth century. R. Hisda also uses a midrashic reading of Job 33:26–27 as his prooftext.

[6] Maimonides, *Mishneh Torah, Laws of Repentance*, 2:9.

[7] There are further steps in both Talmuds in which if the victim has died (not as a result of the offense), the offender must bring ten people to his graveside and apologize there. Finally, the Babylonian Talmud limits the number of apology attempts that are obligatory to three.

[8] Not only asking forgiveness but also granting forgiveness. See Babylonian Talmud Yoma 86b; Maimonides, *Mishneh Torah, Laws of Repentance*, 2:10. On the face-to-face encounter of forgiveness, cf. "Apology, in which the I at the same time asserts itself and inclines before the transcendent, belongs to the essence of conversation (*discours*)." Emmanuel Levinas, *Totality and Infinity: An Essay on Exteriority*, 40.

[9] In addition, a third theory which is a somewhat psychological theory might be called the *closure theory*. This claim (especially in capital cases) is that a punishment must be meted out so that the victim's family can have "closure." Many writers have pointed out the especially slippery and undefined nature of "closure" and therefore its potential for abuse. See Susan Bandes, "Victims, 'Closure,' and the Sociology of Emotion," *Law and Contemporary Problems* 72 (2):1–26.

[10] "Punishment." Encyclopædia Britannica. Encyclopædia Britannica Online. Encyclopædia Britannica, 2010 (August 11, 2010), http://www.search.eb.com/eb/article-272339.

[11] Cf. William Ian Miller, *Eye for an Eye* (Cambridge University Press, 2006) especially chapter 5.

[12] "Restorative justice emphasizes the humanity of both offender and victim, and repair of social connections and peace as more important than retribution." Martha Minow, "Between Vengeance and Forgiveness: Feminist Responses to Violent Injustice," 32 New Eng. L. Rev. 969.

[13] Since the locus of my thinking in this book is the city, in this chapter, I will not be discussing restorative justice in the aftermath of genocide; however, that is one of the very significant directions that it has taken with, for example, the Truth and Reconciliation Commissions in South Africa. On this, see Martha Minow, *Between Vengeance and Forgiveness: Facing History after Genocide and Mass Violence* (Boston, MA: Beacon Press, 1998); Ariel Dorfman, "Whose Memory? Whose Justice? a Meditation on How and When and If to Reconcile," The 8th Mandela Lecture (July 31, 2010) Web. August 11, 2010, http://www.nelsonmandela.org/images/uploads/WHOSE_MEMORY_WHOSE_JUSTICE_final_version_july_2010_for_publication_purposes.pdf.

[14] Cf. Maimonides's explanation for the seriousness of murder (and why, even if a murderer could get off with a technicality, the rabbis created an alternative form of capital punishment): "for even though there are crimes that are worse than murder, none of them have the potential for destroying civilization (*yishuvo shel 'olam*) as murder does." *Laws of Murderers* 4:7.

[15] Maimonides in *Laws of Repentance* writes, "However, transgressions between individuals, such as one who physically damages his fellow or curses his fellow or steals from him, he is not forgiven until he compensates his fellow and appeases him." In Laws of Torts, Maimonides writes, "There is no comparison between the one who injures his fellow bodily to the one who damages his money [or belongings]. One who damages his fellow's money, once he has paid him that which he owes him he is forgiven. However, one who injures his fellow bodily, even though he gives him the five categories of compensation, he is not forgiven. . . . until he asks for forgiveness from the injured party and [the injured party] grants forgiveness." The commentaries to Maimonides take up this contradiction and attempt to smooth it over. See, *inter alia*, Rabbi Abraham de Bouton, *Lehem Mishneh* at *Laws of Torts* 5:9.

[16] The Babylonian Talmud says that the victim can demand that the offender return three times.

[17] See Mishnah Berachot 1:2.

[18] Efraim Elimelech Urbach, *The Sages: Their Concepts and Beliefs,* (Magnes Press, 1969), p. 534 n. 16.

[19] Michael Sokoloff, *a Dictionary of Jewish Babylonian Aramaic of the Talmudic and Geonic Periods*, vol. 3, Dictionaries of Talmud, Midrash, and Targum (Johns Hopkins University Press, 2002), 245.

[20] See the sources cited in Sokoloff, p. 969.

[21] There is an interesting variant reading in two MSS (Munich 95 and Paris 176). These manuscripts don't have this line and instead have: *shamtinhu b'a l'ovdinhu/*

he excommunicated them and sought to destroy them. This, of course, changes the narrative in important ways. According to this narrative, Bruria teaches R. Meir about the proper way to relate to evildoers, i.e., to pray for their well-being, rather than teaching him that evildoers are not essentially evil. My reading therefore is of the story according to the scribal tradition represented by the Florence MS and the *editio priceps*, without making any decision about which, if either, is an "original" version.

[22]   "Parallelism is perhaps the most familiar characteristic of Hebrew poetry." Leland Ryken Tremper Longman III, *The Complete Literary Guide to the Bible* (Zondervan, 1993) p. 251.

[23]   This popular quote was originally coined by Augustine of Hippo as "he should hate the fault, but love the man," in Book XIV:6 of *The City of God*.

[24]   I do not intend this metaphor in a psychological sense, but in the sense of rebuilding relationships and reestablishing the fabric of the community.

[25]   See, for example, John O. Haley, "Comment on Using Criminal Punishment to Serve Both Victim and Social Needs," *Law and Contemporary Problems*, vol. 72 (Spring 2009): 219–225. There is a story in BT Yoma 87a which graphically describes the result of not reintegrating the offender. In that story, the putative offender ends up with a meat cleaver in his head.

[26]   There is no written example of Gandhi's having used the quote, though it is popularly attributed to him. Martin Luther King Jr. used the quote in his 1958 book, *Stride Toward Freedom: The Montgomery Story* (http://quoteinvestigator. com/2010/12/27/eye-for-eye-blind/; accessed February 23, 2011).

[27]   There are two other biblical sources for the Talion: Leviticus 24:18 and Deuteronomy 19:18. It also appears in Roman Law.

[28]   *Laws of Personal Injuries and Damages* 1:3. Maimonides is relying *inter alia* on the discussion in Bavli Baba Kama 83b*ff*.

[29]   David Novak, "Lex Talionis: a Maimonidean Perspective on Scripture, Tradition and Reason," *S'vara: a Journal of Philosophy and Judaism*, vol. 2, no. 1 (1991): 64. See also David Novak, *Covenantal Rights: a Study in Jewish Political Theory* (Princeton University Press: 2000): 161–162.

[30]   *Covenantal Rights*, 162.

[31]   William Ian Miller, *Eye for an Eye* (Cambridge University Press, 2006).

[32]   Cf. "The talion works some quick magic: as soon as you take my eye, in that instant your eye becomes mine; I now possess the entitlement to it. And that entitlement is protected by a property rule. I get to set the price, and you will have to accede to my terms to keep me from extracting it" (Miller, *Eye for an Eye*, p. 50).

[33]   I will be arguing in a minute that this is actually what is troubling the discussion in the Bavli. For now, I will note that this is the exact conversation in the Bavli regarding payment for pain. In that case, the formula for arriving at the

correct payment is how much would the offender pay not to experience the pain he or she had inflicted on the victim (Bavli Baba Kama 85a).

[34]   Cf. Miller, 15. Though as Miller points out, the fact is that the possibility of talion has a threatening aspect to it (I *could* take your eye) and "[t]hat is worth something; it makes the compensatory regime of the talion one that cannot help but keep honor firmly in its sights, for fear is bound up in some nontrivial way with respect and the talionic principle is above all a principle of just compensation" (50).

[35]   The classical discussion of *lex talionis*, discussed here, is in the Babylonian Talmud Baba Kama 83b-84a.

[36]   M Baba Kama 8:1.

[37]   The Mishnah itself is not of a piece and also seems to refer to earlier texts, though here is not the place to lay out the source-critical work. See David Weiss-Halivni, *Mekorot 'U-Masorot: Be'urim Ba-Talmud: Masekhet Bava Kama* (Jerusalem: Magnes Press, Hebrew University, 1993).

[38]   It is obvious, structurally and by content, that the first *sugya* ends before the introduction of the *baraita* quoting R. Dosthai b. Yehudah. In the special issue of *S'vara*, this *baraita* is mistakenly included in the first *sugya*. The translators were probably led astray by following the printed editions in which the mark for the end of a *sugya* ":" was mistakenly placed after the discussion of R. Dosthai b. Yehudah's *baraita*, as is obvious from the manuscripts.

[39]   This whole issue has been exhaustively written about. See David Charles Kraemer, *Reading the Rabbis: The Talmud as Literature* (Oxford University Press, 1996) especially chapter 3. Kraemer's reading of the steps of the argument is consistent with mine; however, he does not fully appreciate the implication of this reading, as his interest is in merely using this *sugya* as another prooftext for his larger argument that "the rabbinic authors want to demonstrate their fundamental independence from scripture" (48).

[40]   The language of R. Dosthai b. Yehudah's statement gives the impression that it is a *midrash halakhah*. We don't however have this midrash in any of the extant collections. (In order to distinguish between the textual layers, I am indenting the *stammaitic* or anonymous editorial statements.)

[41]   This line which is obviously an editorial statement interpolated into a Tannaitic text—the Tannaitic text is Hebrew and the interpolation is Aramaic—is missing in the Hamburg manuscript.

[42]   Baba Kama 83b–84a.

[43]   This is the argument that Novak thinks is "more rational, revealing deeper philosophic implications." He sees this argument as a convincing Rabbinic blow against *lex talionis* because of these "deeper philosophic implications." However, the very next lines in the *sugya* (lines that Novak doesn't deal with) argues against these deeper philosophic implications. See Novak, "Lex Talionis: a Maimonidean Perspective on Scripture, Tradition and Reason," p.63.

[44] It is obvious from this and the next unit that the editor of this discussion raised, challenged, and dismissed the very arguments that Novak think decisively defeat the talionic side (ibid.).

[45] *Treifah* is one who has some manner of terminal or mortal wound or illness. This is analogous to a *treifah* in an animal (Yiddish: *treif*), which makes the animal *unkosher* since it was "already dead." See Babylonian Talmud Tractate Sanhedrin 78a; *Encyclopedia Talmudit*, s.v. *treifah (adam)*.

[46] Which, I will argue in a moment, is actually the penultimate movement.

[47] The Aramaic word *hamara* can mean either donkey or donkey driver.

[48] Or the case.

[49] This whole discussion is generated by the five categories of damages discussed in the first Mishnah of the eighth chapter of Baba Kama: (1) damage, (2) pain and suffering, (3) healing, (4) compensation for labor lost, and (5) humiliation.

[50] Heather C. West, PhD, "Prison Inmates at Midyear 2009—Statistical Tables" (Bureau of Justice Statistics, 2010).

[51] For example, robbery—53%; receiving stolen property—67%; second-degree burglary—62%. "One and Two Year Follow-up Recidivism Rates for All Paroled Felons Released from Prison for the First Time in 2005 under the Supervision of the California Department of Corrections and Rehabilitation" (California Department of Corrections and Rehabilitation Adult Research Branch, 2008).

[52] The Jewish Community Justice Project itself is no longer operating in Los Angeles. For an overview of the current state of restorative justice programs in North America, see Mark S. Umbreit, Betty Vos, Robert B. Coates, Elizabeth Lightfoot, "Restorative Justice in the Twenty-first Century: a Social Movement Full of Opportunities and Pitfalls," *Marquette Law Review* 89:251–304.

Chapter 8

Conclusion

When the great sage Hillel was asked by a stranger to teach him the whole Torah while he stood on one foot, Hillel answered, "That which is hateful to you, do not do to your fellow."[1] When the nineteenth-century rabbi and leader of the Mussar movement, Reb Simhah Zissel of Kelm, sat down to write out the principles of Jewish ethical practice, he began by claiming that the highest level of readying oneself for "acquiring Torah" is sharing with one's fellow their burden, literally helping them carry their burden. "To reach the level of being one who bears the burden of one's fellow is impossible unless one has accustomed oneself to love one's neighbor in thought and deed."[2]

This book is the attempt to take the threads of this tradition of Other-directed ethics, an ethics of the Stranger which is grounded in obligation rather than in symmetrical rights, and first, to make it explicit in its most robust form, and second, to place it in immediate contact with contemporary concerns. I do not claim that this is the only way to read the Jewish textual tradition. I do claim that this reading of the tradition is not episodic but consistent and, hopefully, convincing in such a way that it will also find a home in the public spheres of our conversations about justice.

If you have travelled with me thus far, I hope you have also gathered that the path toward a community of obligation starts in discourse but is dependent on action. Action is always twofold. Individual actions of justice and empathy, such as stopping to talk to a homeless man or giving money or food to a homeless woman, are important even though they do not go very far in changing the political situation wherein there are homeless people. However, it is in the normalizing of intercourse with people who would otherwise be invisible or erased that one can develop the consciousness that is necessary for action on the political level. In a community of obligation, we are all, at all times, attempting to be awake to consequences of our actions.[3]

The just city, the city that is a community of obligation, is a city in which the privilege of residency is obligation. To be a resident of a city means to make yourself accessible to hearing the cry of the Stranger. It also means hearing and seeing the injustice of the Stranger as your own and experiencing that as an obligation to protest against the injustice. It means being awake to the fact that many people live in this city, people who you will not know but are impacted (for good or ill) by your action. I strove to illuminate this general theory of the community of obligation in certain particulars. Homelessness is the undermining of the notion of a city. Labor relations need to be based on an acknowledgment of the humanity and dignity of both worker and employer. This latter means that labor should not be seen as merely the purchase of a commodity from a worker by an employer. Finally, the system of justice itself has to be re-framed such that the end of justice is restoring the community and repairing—to the extent possible—the tear in the fabric of the community that was caused by an offense and an offender.

I have not exhausted the issues that can be specifically addressed within this framework. There are many other issues that need to be thought through—poverty, trafficking in persons, and many more. "The day is short, and the work is plentiful."

There are many people—authors, activists, and author-activists—who have come before me.[4] What I hope to have added is a conceptual framework and a vocabulary that can lay claim to the centuries-old tradition of Rabbinic Judaism and deploy it to address the very real problems that are in front of us, in "the fierce urgency of now."[5]

Notes

[1] Bavli Shabbat 31a.

[2] Simha Zissel Ziv, *Sefer Hochmah 'U-mussar* (New York, 1957) p. 1. The translation is from Ira F. Stone, a *Responsible Life: The Spiritual Path of Mussar* (New York: Aviv Press, 2006), 161.

[3] Emmanuel Levinas, "Cities of Refuge," in *Beyond the Verse: Talmudic Readings and Lectures* (Bloomington, Indiana: Indiana University Press, 1994).

[4] See especially Elliot N. Dorff, *To Do the Right and the Good: a Jewish Approach to Modern Social Ethics* (Jewish Publication Society, 2002); Lenn E. Goodman, *On Justice: An Essay in Jewish Philosophy* (The Littman Library of Jewish Civilization, 2008); Jill Jacobs, *There Shall Be No Needy: Pursuing Social Justice through Jewish Law and Tradition* (Jewish Lights Publishing, 2009).

[5] "We are now faced with the fact that tomorrow is today. We are confronted with the fierce urgency of now. In this unfolding conundrum of life and history there is such a thing as being too late. Procrastination is still the thief of time. Life often leaves us standing bare, naked and dejected with a lost opportunity. The 'tide in the affairs of men' does not remain at the flood; it ebbs. We may cry out desperately for time to pause in her passage, but time is deaf to every plea and rushes on. Over the bleached bones and jumbled residue of numerous civilizations are written the pathetic words: 'Too late.' There is an invisible book of life that faithfully records our vigilance or our neglect. 'The moving finger writes, and having writ moves on . . .' We still have a choice today; nonviolent coexistence or violent co-annihilation." Rev. Martin Luther King Jr. "Beyond Vietnam: a Time to Break the Silence," speech delivered April 4, 1967 at Riverside Church, New York City, http://www.hartford-hwp.com/archives/45a/058.html (accessed August 26, 2010).

BIBLIOGRAPHY

Abulafiah, Meir Halevi. "Yad Ramah." n.d.

Appiah, Kwame Anthony. *Cosmopolitanism: Ethics in a World of Strangers.* New York: W. W. Norton, 2006.

Archibold, Randal C. "Los Angeles to Permit Sleeping on Sidewalks." *New York Times*, October 11, 2007, http://www.nytimes.com/2007/10/11/us/11skidrow.html.

Arietta, R. M. "'Reel Profits, Real Poverty': Security Guards Organize in Hollywood." *In These Times*, February 4, 2010, http://www.inthesetimes.com/working/entry/5510/reel_profits_ reel_poverty_security_guards_organize_in_hollywood/

Aristotle. "The Politics." In *The Penguin Classics*, edited by Thomas Alan Sinclair, 319. Baltimore: Penguin Books, 1962.

Armitt, Lucie. *Theorizing the Fantastic.* London: Arnold, 1996.

Arnold, Kathleen R. *Homelessness, Citizenship, and Identity: The Uncanniness of Late Modernity.* SUNY Series in National Identities. Albany: State University of New York Press, 2004.

Averroes. "Averroes on Plato's Republic." Ithaca: Cornell University Press, 1974.

Ayali, Me'ir. *Po'alim Ve-Omanim: Melakhtam U-Ma'amadam Be-Sifrut Haza"L.* Giv'atayim, Ramat-Gan: Yad la-Talmud, 1987.

Ayali, Meir. *Otsar Kinuye 'Ovdim Be-Sifrut Ha-Talmud Veha-Midrash.* 2nd edition, expanded, "Sifriyat Hilel Hayim." Tel Aviv: Hotsa'at ha-Kibuts ha-me'uhad, 2001.

Bandes, Susan. "Victims, 'Closure,' and the Sociology of Emotion." *Law and Contemporary Problems* 72, no. 2 (2009): 1-26.

Barry, Dan. "Living in Tents, and by the Rules, under a Bridge." *New York Times*, July 31, 2009, http://www.nytimes.com/2009/07/31/us/31land.html.

Ben-Yishai, Ron, Nahum Barnea, and Sever Plocker. "Slavery in Israel?" *Ynet*, http://www.ynetnews.com/articles/0,7340,L-3384268,00.html.

Berkowitz, Beth A. *Execution and Invention: Death Penalty Discourse in Early Rabbinic and Christian Cultures*. Oxford: Oxford University Press, 2006.

Blidstein, Gerald J. "Talmudic Ethics and Contemporary Problematics." *Review of Rabbinic Judaism* 12, no. 2 (2009): 204-17.

Blue Ribbon Commission. "Feeding Our Communities: A Call for Standards for Food Access and Job Quality in Los Angeles' Grocery Industry." Los Angeles: Blue Ribbon Commission on L.A.'s Grocery Industry and Community Health, 2008.

Boyarin, Daniel. *Intertextuality and the Reading of Midrash*. Indiana Studies in Biblical Literature. Bloomington: Indiana University Press, 1990.

------. *Border Lines: The Partition of Judaeo-Christianity*. Philadelphia: University of Pennsylvania Press, 2004.

Brookings Institution. "Restoring America's Promise of Opportunity, Prosperity and Growth." Washington, DC: Brookings Institution, 2006.

Brown, Benjamin. "The Hafetz Hayim on Delayed Wages: Towards a Modernization of Halakhic Labor Law." *Tarbiz* 74, no. 3-4 (2006): 501-38.

Brown, Peter. *Poverty and Leadership in the Later Roman Empire*. Hanover: Brandeis University Press, 2002.

------. "Remembering the Poor and the Aesthetic of Society." *Journal of Interdisciplinary History* 35, no. 3 (2005).

California Department of Corrections and Rehabilitation. "One and Two Year Follow-up Recidivism Rates for All Paroled Felons Released from Prison for the First Time in 2005 under the Supervision of the California Department of Corrections and Rehabilitation." Los Angeles: California Department of Corrections and Rehabilitation Adult Research Branch, 2008.

Chase, Katie Johnston. "A Hard Ending for Housekeepers." *The Boston Globe*, September 17, 2009, http://www.boston.com/business/articles/2009/09/17/housekeepers_lose_hyatt_jobs_to_outsourcing/.

Cohen, Aryeh. "Representation of Death in the Bavli." *AJS Review* 24, no. 1 (1999): 45-71.

Cohen, Mark R. *Poverty and Charity in the Jewish Community of Medieval Egypt*. Princeton: Princeton University Press, 2005.

Confessore, Nichols. "Domestic Workers' Rights Bill Passes." *City Room*, July 1, 2010, http://cityroom.blogs.nytimes.com/2010/07/01/domestic-workers-rights-bill-passes/.

Cover, Robert. "Nomos and Narrative." In *Narrative, Violence, and the Law: The Essays of Robert Cover*, edited by Michael Ryan Martha Minow and Austin Sarat. Ann Arbor: University of Michigan Press, 1992.

------. "The Folktales of Justice: Tales of Jurisdiction." In *Narrative, Violence and the Law*, edited by Michael Ryan Martha Minow and Austin Sarat. Ann Arbor: University of Michigan Press, 1992.

Derrida, Jacques. "On Cosmopolitanism." In his *On Cosmopolitanism and Forgiveness*. London: Routledge, 2001.

Dorff, Elliot N. *To Do the Right and the Good: A Jewish Approach to Modern Social Ethics*, first ed. Philadelphia: Jewish Publication Society, 2002.

Dumon, Peter. "A 'Living Wage' Is Money in the Bank." *Los Angeles Times*, June 11, 2008.

Elman, Yaakov. "Order, Sequence, and Selection: The Mishnah's Anthological Choices." In *The Anthology in Jewish Literature*, edited by David Stern, 53-80. Oxford: Oxford University Press, 2004.

------. "The Babylonian Talmud in Its Historical Context." In *Printing the Talmud: From Bomberg to Schottenstein*, edited by Sharon Lieberman Mintz and Gabriel M. Goldstein. New York: Yeshiva University Museum, 2005.

Feinstein, Moshe. *Igrot Moshe: Hoshen Mishpat*. Vol. I.

Fonrobert, Charlotte Elisheva. *Menstrual Purity: Rabbinic and Christian Reconstructions of Biblical Gender*. Stanford: Stanford University Press, 2000.

------. "The Political Symbolism of the Eruv." *Jewish Social Studies* 11, no. 3 (2005): 9-35.

Foucault, Michel. "A Preface to Transgression." In *Language, Counter-Memory, Practice*, edited by Donald F. Bouchard. Oxford: Basil Blackwell, 1977.

Fox, Everett. *The Five Books of Moses. Genesis, Exodus, Leviticus, Numbers, Deuteronomy: A New Translation with Introductions, Commentary, and Notes*. New York: Schocken Books, 1995.

------. *Give Us a King : Samuel, Saul, and David: A New Translation of Samuel I and II*, first ed. New York: Schocken Books, 1999.

Fox, Everett, and Ivan Schwebel. *The Five Books of Moses: Genesis, Exodus, Leviticus, Numbers, Deuteronomy*, first paperback ed. New York: Schocken Books, 2000.

Friedman, Shamma. *Tosefta Atikata 'Al Masechet Pesach Rishon*. Ramat Gan: 2003.

Friedman, Shamma. *"'Lo Hargu Neheragin, Hargu Eyn Neheragin' (Bavli Makot 5b): Mispah 'O Mishpat?" Sidra* 20 (2005): 171-94.

Gibbs, Robert. "Verdict and Sentence: Cover and Levinas on the Robe of Justice." *Journal of Jewish Thought and Philosophy* 14, no. 1-2 (2006): 73-90.

Goodman, Lenn Evan. *On Justice: An Essay in Jewish Philosophy*. New Haven: Yale University Press, 1991.

Goodman, Lenn E. *On Justice: An Essay in Jewish Philosophy*. Oxford: The Littman Library of Jewish Civilization, 2008.

Haley, John O. "Comment on Using Criminal Punishment to Serve Both Victim and Social Needs." *Law and Contemporary Problems* 72 (2009): 219-25.

Halivni, David. *MeKorot U-Masorot : Be'urim Ba-Talmud: Masekhet Bava Kama*. Jerusalem: Magnes Press and Hebrew University, 1993.

Hasan-Rokem, Galit. *Tales of the Neighborhood: Jewish Narrative Dialogues in Late Antiquity*. Berkeley: University of California Press, 2003.

Hauptman, Judith. *Rereading the Mishnah: A New Approach to Ancient Jewish Texts*. Tubingen, Germany: Mohr Siebeck, 2005.

Helinger, Moshe. "Justice and Social Justice in Halakhic Jusaism and in Current Liberal Thought." In *My Justice, Your Justice: Justice across Cultures*, edited by Yedidia Z. Stern. Jerusalem: Zalman Shazar Center and Israel Democracy Institute, 2010.

Hendricks, Obery. *The Politics of Jesus: Rediscovering the True Revolutionary Nature of Jesus' Teachings and How They Have Been Corrupted*. New York: Doubleday, 2006.

Herzog, Annabel. "Is Liberalism 'All We Need'?: Levinas's Politics of Surplus." *Political Theory* 30, no. 2 (2002): 204-27.

Horovitz, S., and I. A. Rabin. "Mechilta D'rabbi Ismael." Jerusalem: Bamberger & Wahrmann, 1960. P. 360.

Jackson, Bernard S. "Lex Talionis: Revisiting Daube's Classic." Brigham Young University Law School. http://www.law2.byu.edu/Biblical_Law/papers/jackson_bs_lex_talionis.pdf.

Jacobs, Jill. *There Shall Be No Needy: Pursuing Social Justice through Jewish Law & Tradition*, hardcover ed. Woodstock, VT: Jewish Lights, 2009.

Kraemer, David Charles. *Reading the Rabbis: The Talmud as Literature*. Oxford: Oxford University Press, 1996.

Levinas, Emmanuel. *Totality and Infinity: An Essay on Exteriority*. Translated by Alphonso Lingis. Pittsburgh: Duquesne University Press, 1969.

------. "Cities of Refuge." In his *Beyond the Verse: Talmudic Readings and Lectures*, translated by Gary D. Mole. Bloomington: Indiana University Press, 1994.

Levinstam, Shmuel Efraim. "'Eglah 'Arufah." In *Encyclopaedia Biblica*, edited by Eleazar Lipa Sukenik, Umberto Cassuto, 77-78. Jerusalem: Mosad Bialik, 1950.

Loewenberg, Frank M. *From Charity to Social Justice: The Emergence of Communal Institutions for the Support of the Poor in Ancient Judaism*. New Brunswick: Transaction Publishers, 2001.

Los Angeles Homeless Services Authority. "2007 Greater Los Angeles Homeless Count Report." Los Angeles: Los Angeles Homeless Services Authority, 2007.

Los Angeles Homeless Services Authority. "2009 Greater Los Angeles Homeless Count Report." Los Angeles: Los Angeles Homeless Services Authority, 2009.

Lossing, Ben. *Harper's New Monthly Magazine* (1856).

MacIntyre, Alasdair C. *Whose Justice? Which Rationality?* Notre Dame, IN: University of Notre Dame Press, 1988.

Maimonides, Moses. *The Guide of the Perplexed*. Edited by Shlomo Pines. Chicago: University of Chicago Press, 1974.

Maus, Macel. *The Gift: Forms and Functions of Exchange in Archaic Societies*. Translated by Ian Cunnison. New York: Norton, 1967.

Meiri, Menahem ben Solomon. "Beth Habehira on the Talmudical Treatise Shabbath." Edited by Isaak S Lange, 16, 620. Jerusalem: 1968.

Milgrom, Jacob. *Leviticus 1-16: A New Translation with Introduction and Commentary*, first ed. New York: Doubleday, 1991.

Milkman, Ruth, Ana Luz Gonzalez, and Victor Narro. *Wage Theft and Workplace Violations in Los Angeles: The Failure of Employment and Labor Law for Low-Wage Workers*. Los Angeles: UCLA Institute for Research on Labor and Employment, 2010.

Millar, Fergus. *The Roman Near East: 31 B.C.-A.D. 337*. Cambridge, MA: Harvard University Press, 1994.

Miller, Fred. "Aristotle's Political Theory." In *The Stanford Encyclopedia of Philosophy*, edited by Edward N. Zalta. Stanford: Stanford University, 2010.

Miller, William Ian. *Eye for an Eye*. Cambridge: Cambridge University Press, 2006.

Minow, Martha. "Between Vengeance and Forgiveness: Feminist Responses to Violent Injustice." *New England Law Review* 32 (1998): 967-81.

------. *Between Vengeance and Forgiveness: Facing History after Genocide and Mass Violence*. Boston: Beacon Press, 1998.

Mishnah. London: Oxford University Press, 1933.

Nadasen, Premilla. "Domestic Worker Bill of Rights Passes New York Senate." *Ms. Blog Magazine,* June 4, 2010, http://msmagazine.com/blog/blog/2010/06/04/domestic-worker-bill-of-rights-passes-new-york-senate/

National Law Center on Homelessness and Poverty, National Coalition for the Homeless. "Homes Not Handcuffs: The Criminalization of Homelessness in U.S. Cities." Washington, DC: National Law Center on Homelessness and Poverty and National Coalition for the Homeless, 2009.

Novak, David. "Lex Talionis: A Maimonidean Perspective on Scripture, Tradition and Reason." *S'vara: A Journal of Philosophy and Judaism* 2, no. 1 (1991).

------. *Covenantal Rights: A Study in Jewish Political Theory*. Princeton: Princeton University Press, 2000.

Nussbaum, Martha. *Frontiers of Justice: Disability, Nationality and Species Membership*. Cambridge, MA: Harvard University Press, 2007.

Page, Samantha. "Former Employees Protest Marina Car Wash's Abrupt Firings." *Venice Patch*, December 15, 2010, http://venice.patch.com/articles/former-employees-protest-marina-car-washs-abrupt-firings.

Peskowitz, Miriam B. *Spinning Fantasies: Rabbis, Gender and History*. Berkeley: University of California Press, 1997.

Rawls, John. *A Theory of Justice*, rev. ed. Cambridge, MA: Belknap Press of Harvard University Press, 1999.

Rubenstein, Jeffrey L. *The Culture of the Babylonian Talmud*. Baltimore: Johns Hopkins University Press, 2003.

Ryken, Leland, and Tremper Longman III. *A Complete Literary Guide to the Bible.* Grand Rapids, MI: Zondervan, 1993.

Searle, John R. "Social Ontology and Political Power." In his *Free Will and Neurobiology: Reflections on Free Will, Language and Political Power.* New York: Columbia University Press, 2007.

Segal, Alan. *Rebecca's Children: Judaism and Christianity in the Roman World.* Cambridge, MA: Harvard University Press, 1986.

Septimus, Bernard. *Hispano-Jewish Culture in Transition: The Career and Controversies of Ramah.* Cambridge, MA: Harvard University Press, 1982.

Shiffman, Lawrence. "The Making of the Mishnah and the Talmud." In *Printing the Talmud: From Bomberg to Schottenstein,* edited by Sharon Lieberman Mintz and Gabriel M. Goldstein. New York: Yeshiva University Museum, 2005.

Singer, Peter. "What Should a Billionaire Give - and What Should You?" *New York Times,* December 17, 2006, http://www.nytimes.com/2006/12/17/magazine/17charity.t.html?pagewanted=all.

Sokoloff, Michael. *A Dictionary of Jewish Babylonian Aramaic of the Talmudic and Geonic Periods.* Vol. 3, Dictionaries of Talmud, Midrash, and Targum. Baltimore: Johns Hopkins University Press, 2002.

Stone, Ira F. *A Responsible Life: The Spiritual Path of Mussar.* New York: Aviv Press, 2006.

Stout, Jeffrey. *Democracy and Tradition.* Princeton: Princeton University Press, 2004.

Theodor, Julius, and Chanoch Albeck. "Midrash Bereshit Rabba: Critical Edition with Notes and Commentary." Jerusalem: Wahrmann Books, 1965.

Todorov, Tzvetan. *The Fantastic: A Structural Approach to a Literary Genre.* Ithaca, NY: Cornell, 1980.

Torok, Ryan. "Rabbi, AJU Professor Arrested at Hotel Workers Protest." *Jewish Journal,* July 23, 2010, http://www.jewishjournal.com/community/article/rabbi_aju_professor_arrested_at_hotel_workers_protest_20100723/

Umbreit, Mark S., Betty Vos, Robert B. Coates, and Elizabeth Lightfoot. "Restorative Justice in the Twenty-First Century: A Social Movement Full of Opportunities and Pitfalls." *Marquette Law Review* 89 (2004): 251-304.

Bibliography

United States Court of Appeals for the Ninth Circuit. *Edward Jones; Patricia Vinson; George Vinson; Thomas Cash; Stanley Barger; Robert Lee Purrie, Plaintiffs-Appellants, v. City of Los Angeles; William Bratton, Chief; Charles Beck, Captain, in Their Official Capacity, Defendants-Appellees.* Pasadena, CA: 2006.

Urbach, Efraim Elimelech. *The Sages: Their Concepts and Beliefs.* Jerusalem: Magnes Press, 1969.

Urban Land Institute. "Mixed Income Housing Advisory Group: Workforce Housing Options in Los Angeles Considerations for the City of Los Angeles (Draft)." Los Angeles: Urban Land Institute, 2008.

Uzziel, Ben-Zion Meir Chai. *Mishpetei Uziel.* Vol. IV, *Hoshen Mishpat.* n.d.

Walker, Rob. "The Born Identity." *The New York Times*, August 1, 2010, http://www.nytimes.com/2010/08/01/magazine/01fob-consumed-t. html.

Weiss, Ruhama. *Mithayevet Benafshy: Kri'ot Mehuyavot Batalmud*: Yediot Ahronot, 2006.

West, Heather C. "Prison Inmates at Midyear 2009-Statistical Tables." Bureau of Justice Statistics, 2010.

Wyschogrod, Edith. *Saints and Postmodernism: Revisioning Moral Philosophy.* Chicago: University of Chicago Press, 1990.

------. "The Challenge of Justice: The Ethics of 'Upbuilding'." In *Kierkegaard and Levinas: Ethics, Politics, and Religion*, edited by J. Aaron Simmons and David Wood, 199-210. Bloomington: Indiana University Press, 2008.

Index

Index of Biblical and Talmudic Sources

CPSIA information can be obtained at www.ICGtesting.com
Printed in the USA
LVOW07s1446310713

345582LV00002B/126/P

9 781618 112965